Token Ring
Network Design

Data Communications and Networks Series

Consulting Editor: Dr C. Smythe, University of Sheffield

Selected titles

Token Ring
Network Design

David Bird

Proteon International

ADDISON-WESLEY
PUBLISHING
COMPANY

Wokingham, England • Reading, Massachusetts • Menlo Park, California • New York
Don Mills, Ontario • Amsterdam • Bonn • Sydney • Singapore
Tokyo • Madrid • San Juan • Milan • Paris • Mexico City • Seoul • Taipei

The programs in this book have been included for their instructional value. They have been tested with care but are not guaranteed for any particular purpose. The publisher does not offer any warranties or representations nor does it accept any liabilities with respect to the programs.

Many of the designations used by manufacturers and sellers to distinguish their products are claimed as trademarks. Addison-Wesley has made every attempt to supply trademark information about manufacturers and their products mentioned in this book. A list of the trademark designations and their owners appears below.

Cover designed by Chris Eley
and printed by The Riverside Printing Co. (Reading) Ltd.
Typeset by Colset Pte Ltd, Singapore
Printed and bound in Great Britain by T. J. Press (Padstow) Ltd, Padstow, Cornwall

First printed 1994

ISBN 0–201–62760–4

British Library Cataloguing-in-Publication Data
A catalogue record for this book is available from the British Library.

Library of Congress Cataloging-in-Publication Data applied for.

Trademark Notice

Proteon®, Pronet® are registered trademarks of Proteon Inc.
IBM™, PC XT™, PC AT™, MCA™, OS/2™, PS/2™, Token Ring™ are trademarks of International Business Machines Corporation.
Intel®, Multibus® are registered trademarks of Intel Corporation.
Texas Instruments®, TI® are registered trademarks of Texas Instruments.
Banyan®, Vines® are registered trademarks of Banyan Incorporated.
Novell®, NetWare® are registered trademarks of Novell Incorporated.
Microsoft®, LAN Manager® are registered trademarks of Microsoft Corporation.
AT&T®, Systimax® are registered trademarks of American Telephone and Telegraph Company.
Sun® is a registered trademark of Sun Corporation.
Bell™ is a trademark of Bell Labs.
Apollo™ is a trademark of Apollo Corporation.
DECnet™ is a trademark of Digital Equipment Corporation.

Preface

This book is intended as a guide to planning, configuring and installing IEEE 802.5 compatible Local Area Networks (LANs). It will help you to determine the hardware, software and communication media required to interconnect your computers.

The book is suitable for anyone who is planning, considering or maintaining an IEEE 802.5 network, including system administrators, network planners, network managers, facilities managers, telecommunications engineers, resellers and network maintenance personnel.

The book is organized as follows:

	summarizes the rules and formulae used in the main chapters
Appendix C	Includes forms and worksheets that can help with the network design
Glossary	Defines the most common terms used in networking
Index	An alphabetical list of the main items discussed in this guide.

This book should be used in conjunction with the data sheets and manuals supplied by the vendor and/or manufacturer of your Token Ring products. Data sheets will be helpful as an overview when planning and configuring a network; configuration and installation manuals will be required during installation and commissioning.

David Bird
April, 1994

Contents

1

Introduction to Token Ring networks

Chapter summary

In the early 1970s a technology emerged that enabled several computer users to 'share' a cable in order to access the computer. This provided significant savings in cabling costs and offered greater flexibility for connecting devices than was previously possible. The new system, which uses a single coaxial cable, is commonly known as **Ethernet**.

In the early 1980s another technology emerged, with the same ability to reduce cabling costs, but instead of requiring coaxial cable it utilized **shielded twisted pair** cabling. This 'newer' technology also offered the potential for higher performance, improved security and more flexible designs. It is known as **Token Ring** and networks using this technology are deemed **Token Ring networks**. The term is derived from the method of operation and the way that terminals (or

1

nodes) are linked together. The nodes are connected from one to another to form a **ring** and a specific pattern of data – a **token** – is used to decide which node can use the ring at any one time.

Whilst the main purpose of this book is to enable you to design Token Ring networks, Chapter 1 attempts to set the scene with a brief introduction to the 4 and 16 **Mbps** Token Ring technologies as defined by the respective standards body. This is the **Institute of Electrical and Electronic Engineers (IEEE)** of the USA whose '800 series' of recommendations relate to networks in general and which defines Token Ring standards in the **IEEE 802.5** series specifications, in particular.

Chapter 1 first outlines the concepts and operation of a token passing arbitration system, used to control access to the shared **media**, and compares this with the **broadcast** and collision detection method used by Ethernet. It then looks at the early 4 Mbps Token Ring technology, particularly the reclocking and retiming methods and the maintenance features built into the network circuits (or chips), illustrating why and how they affect the network design.

The chapter concludes by considering the additional features of the current 4/16 Mbps (switchable) chipsets, in particular the functions that must be considered when designing networks to operate at 16 Mbps.

1.1   Overview

Token Ring networks are not new. Rather, recent advancements in technology and endorsements by the respective Standards Organizations have made them acceptable. You could say that 'Token Rings have grown up'. Today this technology gives us more functionality, better performance and greater control of our networks than ever before and all at a reasonable price.

Today people want to install Token Ring Local Area Networks (LANs) to connect together their PCs, workstations, **file servers**, **gateways**, and many other systems, as long as there is an interface for it. Unfortunately not everyone is familiar enough with the way Token Rings work (and the factors that have to considered) to be able to design reliable networks to the same extent as with the main alternative – Ethernet. This book is aimed at redressing the balance by

providing a simple set of rules and guidelines to enable you to design
virtually any sized Token Ring – up to the recommended limits, of
course!

1

Before we look at Token Ring network design let us go back a
little way in history, to the dawn of networking – less than 50 years
ago for this technology – and look briefly at how networks evolved.
We will then spend some time looking at today's Token Ring networks
and how, in basic terms, a Token Ring network works.

A brief history

Local area network technology has its beginnings, so the story goes,
many years ago in far off lands in the middle of the Pacific Ocean
– the Hawaiian Islands actually. Here the inhabitants needed a
reliable yet inexpensive communications system, able to span the long
distances between the islands. They settled on a shared radio system
with contended access, where everyone had a transmitter/receiver
tuned to the same frequency. When anyone wanted to make a call
they would press the transmit button on the radio and say something
like:

'Aloha, aloha!'

and if anyone was listening, they would answer. Everyone heard the
call and could listen to the conversation if they wanted to. It may not
have been very private but it worked and was cheap and easy to
manage.

From this ALOHA network (as it became popularly known) grew
the concepts for what today is called Ethernet, a broadcast network
sharing a common medium in much the same way as the ALOHA
net. Ethernet grew as a commercial product during the mid 1970s,
was very popular in the 1980s – reflecting the explosion in PC sales
– and is still widely used today. Indeed it has the largest installed base
of the two major LAN types, although Token Ring networks are gaining fast.

In its original form Ethernet used coaxial cable as the shared
transmisson medium whilst Token Ring used shielded twisted pair.
The objective was the same in both cases – to reduce costs and complexity by simplifying and reducing the amount of cable required to
interconnect **hosts** (computers usually). In fact this 'shared medium'
method of interconnection and the resulting savings in cable costs
were compelling reasons for computer users to think about installing
a local area network.

Today, advances in technology enable us to support higher and higher data rates over lower grade (hence lower cost) cable – typically unshielded. In addition cables are now available which have been designed to support LAN speeds but still at a reasonable price. This has led to a move back towards star-wired networks; a trend that has been further encouraged by the emergence of **wiring concentrators** and intelligent hubs, which combine port density with management and several other features which can only be provided cost-effectively if they are centralized.

Each topology has advantages and disadvantages and often the choice between a distributed wiring system and a centralized wiring system will depend on the application or even the building/site. The good news is that the recommendations and rules we shall shortly go on to discuss are applicable to either or both topologies.

Let us look at the next stage in the history of Token Ring development, as we now know it, by considering the role of standards.

Standards

One of the driving forces that increases the take-up of any technology is world-wide standards. There are official standards for Token Ring and Ethernet. These are determined and controlled by the Institute of Electrical and Electronic Engineers (IEEE), in the USA, from input, discussion and approval by committees. The network standards are defined by the IEEE 800-series where IEEE 802.5 is the Token Ring standard and IEEE 802.3 defines the standards for what everyone refers to as Ethernet.

This has not always been the case. Whilst Ethernet was gaining dominance in the early 1980s, alternative topologies and network access methods were emerging. Apollo with their 12 Mbps token passing access topology and logical ring connection, called Domain; Proteon with their 10 Mbps Token Passing access topology and similar logical ring, called ProNET-10; and, in Europe, the Cambridge ring, were amongst the most well known.

Despite the success of these products, however, it was not until IBM endorsed the Token Passing Access Method which, in the mid 1980s became the basis for the IEEE 802.5 Token Ring standard of today, that Token Ring networks really 'took off'.

Let us now briefly examine the main characteristics of these two technologies, Ethernet and Token Ring.

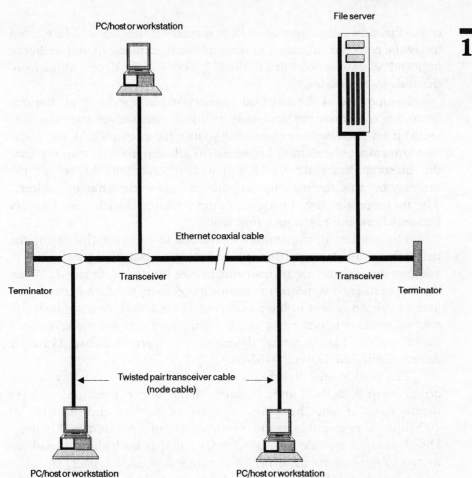

Figure 1.1 Traditional CSMA/CD (Ethernet) topology using coaxial cable with hosts connected via transceivers and twisted pair node cables. One host at a time can transmit and all hosts listen whilst transmitting. Collisions occur when two hosts attempt to transmit at the same time. When a collision is detected, both nodes stop transmitting. Retransmission will start a short, random time later, to avoid further collisions.

Ethernet

The principle of Ethernet is that the hosts, or nodes, share (that is, are connected to) a common medium. This was originally coaxial cable (coax), similar to, but of a heavier gauge than, domestic television or radio coax: known as thick coax it was almost always coloured yellow. Physical access to this coax is via a transceiver on the coax and multipair 'drop' cable from the node, as shown in Figure 1.1.

An alternative lighter gauge coax could be used for smaller groups of nodes spanning shorter distances; this was known as thin coax. Physical access to this coax is directly to the node. More often today the coax has migrated to become the **backplane** of an intelligent hub and all connections are realized by equivalent **drop cables** from the hub to the nodes.

Irrespective of the physical connection, in operation all stations listen for transmissions and only transmit themselves (use the network) if no one else is transmitting (using the network). When a station transmits, the data is broadcast to all stations. All stations hear the message but only the designated receiver should accept the message because the message will have a unique **destination** address. The message also has a unique sender's address so that the receiver knows where the message came from.

The sender or transmitter continues to monitor (listen to) the network whilst transmitting in order to detect the possibility of another sender starting to transmit before theirs has finished. When this happens (two stations transmitting together) the data is corrupted and a collision is said to have occurred. This access and transmission control method is described in lay terms as *Listen before sending/listen whilst sending*. The technical description is **Carrier Sense Multiple Access/Collision Detect** (CSMA/CD).

The advantages of Ethernet are that it uses a relatively simple access control method and, because of the shared medium, reduces media costs. From the point of view of performance it runs at 10 Mbps, a reasonable trade-off in terms of cost and technology. Disadvantages include lack of security, as it is basically a broadcast network, limitations in terms of distance and packet sizes, in order to ensure that collisions can be detected, and the potential performance degradation under heavy traffic as the number of collisions (and hence **retries**) increases.

Token Ring

Token Ring topologies continued the trend of sharing the transmission medium but differed from Ethernet in the critical area of the access method by regulating who can use the cable and when. The type of medium, and how it is used, also differed slightly, partly as a result of the token passing access method and partly by the (initial) proprietary nature of the systems. It comprised two cable pairs, as opposed to a single coax. One pair was used to connect to the previous node and the second pair was used to connect to the next node, as shown in Figure 1.2. A complete ring is formed when the last node is connected back to the first. Shielded twisted pair cabling

1

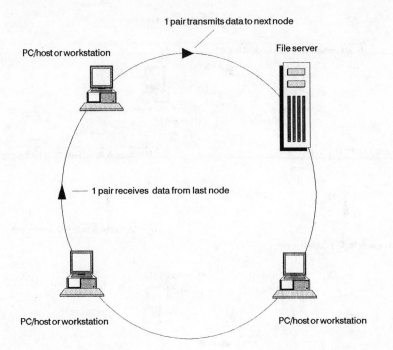

Token ring frame format

SDEL 1 byte	AC 1 byte	FC 1 byte	Destination address 6 bytes	Source address 6 bytes	Message field	FCS 4 bytes	EDEL 1 byte	FS 1 byte

SDEL : Start delimiter
AC   : Access control field
FC   : Frame control field
FCS   : Frame check sequence field
EDEL : End delimiter
FS   : Frame status field (Bits 1 and 5 = frame copied)

Token ring token format

SDEL 1 byte	AC 1 byte	FC 1 byte

Figure 1.2 Token Ring topology and frame format. Token Ring networks can be constructed with two separate cables to every node, to make a physical ring. Manchester encoding is deliberately modified (violations) to distinguish the token from any other bit pattern.

was used to support separate transmit and receive pairs with comparable levels of noise immunity and **drive distances** to those of coax.

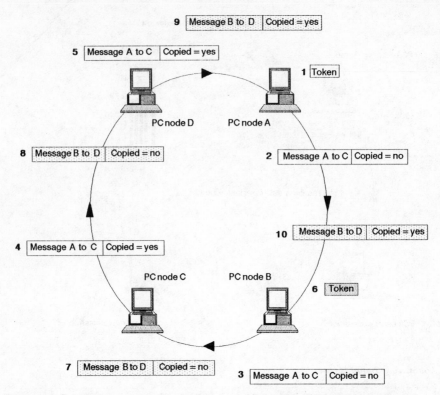

Figure 1.3 Token passing at 4 Mbps operation. The sequence of events is as follows:

(1) PC node A receives and holds the free token
(2) Node A transmits the message A to C
(3) Node B passes the message on
(4) Node C receives the message and sets the frame copied bits
(5) Node A receives own message and strips frame

(6) Node A releases token
(7) Node B holds token and sends message B to D
(8) Node C passes message on
(9) Node D receives message and sets frame copied bits
(10) Node B receives own message and strips frame.

In order to transmit data from one station, or node, to another the sender must first seize the token; this is a unique series of bits or frames that continuously circulate on the ring, passing from one station to the next, controlling access. In this way the token ensures no two stations can transmit at the same time. All stations in the ring can (and do) receive the token, but only one station – the one that holds the token – can transmit at any one time (see Figure 1.3).

This avoids the possibility of data collisions because there is only ever one token. No two stations can transmit simultaneously as a result of this controlled access method. As we shall see later on in this

chapter, there are ways of increasing response times (and hence performance) by doing clever things with the token (that is, early token
release), but there is still only ever one token so only one station can
transmit at a time.

The performance of a Token Ring network is determined by the
time it takes the token to go round the ring – a measure of how long
you may have to wait for access – and the length of the data packets
each station transmits when it has the token, that is, the transmit
delay. For a given ring size (number of nodes) and a maximum packet
size it is possible to calculate the maximum delay for any one station
before it could receive the token and transmit its data. Consequently,
Token Ring networks are often described as deterministic and can be
used in applications requiring a real time response, where Ethernet
cannot.

Let us now look briefly at how data is transmitted on a Token
Ring.

1.2   How does a Token Ring work?

Let us consider a four-node network as shown in Figure 1.3. Node
A wants to send data to node C and Node B wants to send data to
Node D. The token will be circulating on the ring and will be available to use (marked as free or the priority set to a user level). Let us
assume that node A is the next station reached by the circulating
token.

Node A wants to send data:

- Node A will 'hold' the token and transmit a packet onto the
  ring with the format: destination address, source address and
  then data. There will also be starting delimiters, error checking and so on for housekeeping, but most important are the
  frame copied bits, which are used to indicate correct receipt
  of the message, as shown in Figure 1.2.

- The data will be received by node B, which reads the destination address and, because the data is not for this node (B),
  passes the data back out onto the ring unmodified. In fact the
  data is processed 'on-the-fly' to minimize the delay through
  the node interface – typically a one-bit delay.

- The data will be received by node C, which reads the destination address. Because the data is for this node (C), it
  - copies the data to its internal buffers (and eventually to the host memory),
  - passes the data back out onto the ring,
  - and, most important, sets the frame copied bits.
- The modified packet goes through node D in the same way as node B without any further changes.
- When the packet is received back by node A, it reads the destination and source addresses. It is expecting a packet back because *it* is the current active transmitting node. It recognizes the source address as the valid packet it transmitted and removes the packet from the ring.
- Node A also checks the frame copied bits to check that the frame was received correctly. (If not it will contend for the token again to retransmit the packet later.)
- Node A then releases the token.

To improve response times the transmitting node will release the token as soon as it starts stripping the received data from the ring.

- Node B will then receive the token and hold it. Node B will then transmit its data onto the ring. This will be read by node C but not copied as the destination address is that of node D.
- The data will be received by node D which will recognize the destination address and copy the message to its own buffer memory, set the frame copied bits and pass the message back onto the ring.
- Node A will pass this message straight through.

The message will now be received by Node B which will begin to strip the data from the ring and, at the same time, release the token. Once the message has been confirmed as one sent by node B and received correctly, the higher level software will be informed that the transmission was successful. If, for any reason, it was not, node B will wait for the token in order to carry out the retransmit request from the software (usually).

The free token then circulates round the ring once more.

Note that any unknown data on the ring – resulting from a node failure during transmission, a cable fault, or any other cause – will

1

be stripped (removed) from the ring by the next node wanting to transmit, as soon as it receives the token. In this way the ring is always kept clean and made clean prior to any new transmission. Similarly, if the token is lost or destroyed because of a fault condition, the first token-present timer that times-out (all cards have this timer) will generate a new token and transmit it to the ring.

These management functions are built into the electronics (chipsets) which implement the IEEE 802.5 standard; they are known as **Media Access Control** (MAC) functions. They are an integral part of the technology and are transparent to the user. They increase the reliability of modern Token Ring networks. Many of these features are available to, and can be controlled by, specific management software – if it has been designed to access these management functions via the **MAC frames**.

We will be looking at other MAC frames later on in this chapter, and in later chapters, where they are applicable to Token Ring designs. For a more detailed explanation of these and other MAC functions, refer to the **TMS 380** Adapter Chipset – User Guide, referenced in the bibliography, or to the IEEE 802.5 specifications.

Early token release

It is possible to get improved response and performance on the Token Ring by releasing the token *before* the transmitting node has received its own packet back from the ring. This gives rise to the concept of 'multiple packets' on the ring at the same time and manifests itself as the ability to support multiple simultaneous use of the ring or multiple users on the ring.

In fact it is relatively simple to achieve technically because all data is synchronously clocked once on the ring. Data goes round the ring in one direction only and no two packets ever meet. All packets include the source and destination addresses so each node is able to differentiate packets to copy or pass on.

The ability to release the token before data has been received back is called early token release and *is only supported at 16 Mbps operation* where performance is more critical. Again this is a function of the chipset and is transparent to the user. In essence it works as follows.

As before, assume that node A wants to transmit to node C and node B wants to transmit to node D, as shown in Figure 1.4.

- Node A receives the token. It holds the token and sends its data to node B.

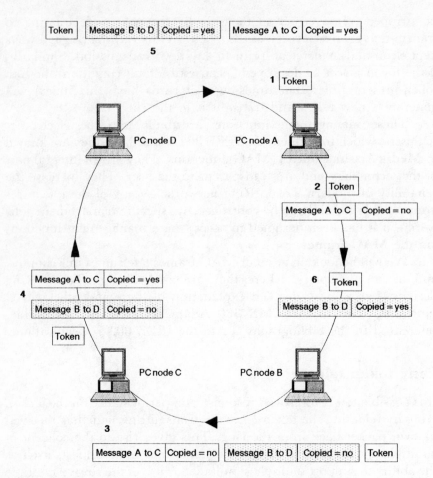

Figure 1.4   Token passing at 16 Mbps – early token release. The sequence is as follows:

(1) Node A receives and holds the free token
(2) Node A sends the message A to C then releases the token
(3) Node B passes A's message on, holds the token, sends message B to D and then releases the token
(4) Node C copies message A to C, sets frame copied bits, passes message and token on
(5) Node D copies the message B to D, sets frame copied bits, passes message and token on
(6) Node A has stripped its own message; passes B's message and token on for B to strip its own message.

1

- A short time after the last bit of data has left node A, node A releases the token.

We now have node A to C data on the ring followed by the token!

- Node B receives the data, reads the destination address, and passes it on as before.
- Next, node B receives the token (there is never more than one). Node B also wants to transmit (to D) so it now holds the token and starts to send its data.

Note that because the token was delayed slightly by node A, there is no possibility that the data node B now sends on the ring will collide with any part of node A's data because node B had to wait for the token before it could start to transmit.

- After node B has finished sending its message on the ring, it will, in turn, wait a short time and then release the token.

We now have three sets of data on the ring: the message node A to C, the message node B to D and the token.

- The first message reaches node C, which copies the data and sets the frame copied bits as this message is addressed to node C. The second message is passed on, as is the token since node C does not want to send any data at this time.
- The first message then reaches node D which passes it on. The second message then reaches node D, which copies the data and sets the frame copied bits as the message is addressed to this node. The token (received next) is also passed on as node D does not want to send any data at this time.

The first message is then received back at node A which, because it is expecting to receive its own message, strips the data from the ring. Node A checks the source address (and frame copied bits) to verify that this is its own message so that it can send a success or failure statement to the higher order software. Node A always strips the first received message (as before) from the ring because it will either be its own message or rubbish. The message should be its own because of the sequential nature of putting messages onto the ring (i.e. first on, first off). If for any reason it is rubbish, this ensures that node B's message is the next message to reach node B.

- Node B next receives the message and similarly strips the data from the ring, verifying the source address and frame copied status.

The token continues to circulate until the next node wants to transmit, unless a special application needs higher access privileges. All this is fully transparent to the user.

As you can probably see, by taking this example further, it is possible for every active node (connected to the ring and able to transmit/receive data) to send data at what appears to be the same time, on a 16 Mbps ring. This is indeed the case; but in practice every node will have some access delay (usually imperceptible to the user) and all messages will be separated in time. However, unless under heavy load, we do not normally see more than two or three users on a ring at any one time.

1.3   Logical vs physical ring topology

We can see from the above examples and the type of cable that Token Ring networks use (twisted pair), that data flows round the ring in one direction only. Each node receives data in one direction on one pair and transmits it to the next node on a second pair. We could cable up the nodes (usually PCs) using two separate cables in this fashion to realize a physical 'ring', but this has two major disadvantages:

- separate cables have to be run between each node (PC),
- it is very difficult to add and delete nodes.

Another problem is that all nodes must be *on* and forwarding packets (said to be in-ring) if the ring is to stay *up*.

During the development of Token Rings it was easy to address these issues by centralizing all node connections in a cabling access unit, forming the 'heart' of the ring, and to use relays to connect and disconnect nodes under the user's control. Today the access units are called **wire centres, Multistation Access Units** (MAUs), **hubs** or **concentrators**. They are available in many different forms depending on the manufacturer, number of nodes, functionality (dumb or

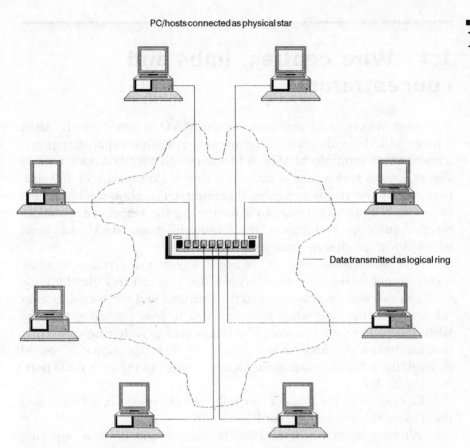

PC/hosts connected as physical star

Data transmitted as logical ring

Figure 1.5 Logical ring using a physical star topology. The wiring concentrator (hub) acts as a physical attachment for nodes in a star configuration but signal (data) flows from node to node as a Token Ring.

intelligent) and mounting (free-standing, rack mounted or integrated with other products).

The cable to the node now becomes one multi-pair (usually two pair) cable. The transmit and receive pairs are run in a single sheath. Each node is connected to the central hub by this cable (the node cable) to realize a topology that is a physical **star** but a logical ring. See Figure 1.5.

Let us now consider these hubs.

1.4   Wire centres, hubs and concentrators

The most widely used and best known MAU is based on the IBM
8-node MSAU with single **ring-in** and **ring-out** expansion ports.
These enable multiple MAUs to be connected together, as shown in
Figure 1.6, to give a maximum single ring node capacity of 260 connections. Whilst the design rules illustrated in this book can be applied
to any hub or concentrator, by substituting the respective manufacturer's figures in the formula, the standard 8-node MSAU has been
adopted for the design examples.

The wire centre node ports are designed using relays to allow
nodes access to the ring (now within the wire centre) via the node
cable. In essence the relays switch the transmit and receive pairs from
the node *into* the ring when a node wants to join and *out of* the ring
when the node wants to leave. The relays also provide ring continuity
because, when the node is not actively in-ring, the signal is routed
through the relay (bypassing the inactive node) to the next node port.
See Figure 1.7.

Operation of the relay is controlled by the node via software and
the Token Ring interface card in the PC.

When a node wants to join the ring it will issue a join ring
command (passed over the phantoms of the signal pairs in the node
cable) which will cause the corresponding node port relay in the wire
centre to switch the node into the ring. Similarly, releasing the join
ring signal, or sending a leave ring signal, will cause the relay to
return to its original status (fall back), taking the node out of the
ring and at the same time bypassing the node to maintain ring
continuity.

We can therefore see that the centralized wire centre concept,
with relay control of the node ports, enables us easily and reliably
to:

- add and remove nodes without disrupting the network,
- connect nodes via a single multi-pair (typically two-pair)
  cable,
- reconfigure and expand the networks via the expansion ports.

Several manufacturers also include relay protection on the expansion
ports (ring-in and ring-out) to detect and isolate any faults on the cable

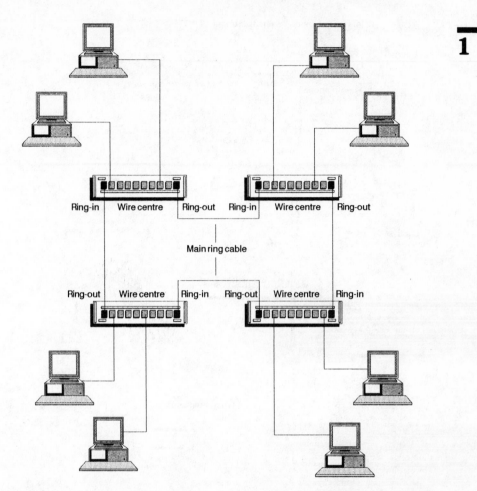

Figure 1.6 MAUs connect together via the ring-in and ring-out ports. The 8-node MAUs are linked together by connecting the ring-out of one unit to the ring-in of the next. The last unit can be connected back to the first unit to form a physical ring of MAUs with the hosts star-connected on each MAU.

between wire centres, the main ring cable or the backbone. A sense current is used to monitor continuity on this main ring cable. In the event of a cable break, the relays fall back, maintaining the ring in loopback mode within the wire centres either side of the fault. This gives additional reliability but does not affect network design.

Whilst there will be differences between the features, functionality and capacities of wire centres, hubs and concentrators from different manufacturers, these will not change the application of the design concepts introduced in this book. All features and functions that are directly related to the IEEE 802.5 specification will be independent of the hub manufacturer, enabling you to use this book to design your Token Ring networks and then, if necessary, adapt the

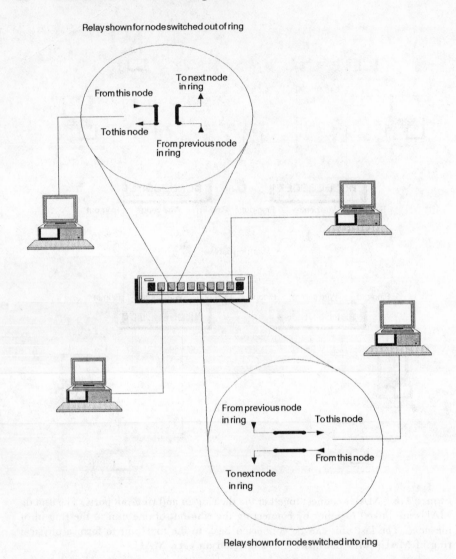

Relay shown for node switched out of ring

To next node in ring

From this node

To this node

From previous node in ring

From previous node in ring

To this node

From this node

To next node in ring

Relay shown for node switched into ring

Figure 1.7 Relay access to the Token Ring via node ports. Node port relays protect the integrity of the ring. Relays are set to loop-through in the MAU and loopback on the node cable when the node is not 'in-ring'. (Relays are shown simplified to demonstrate the principle of operation.)

topology to suit the specific manufacturer's products.

To complete this introduction to the technology of Token Rings, although not strictly necessary for their design, we look at some of the key MAC frames and error conditions, particularly beaconing. We will then complete Chapter 1 by introducing some considerations for 16 Mbps network designs. They are addressed in more detail in later chapters.

1.5   MAC frames and design

Wire centres give rise to a physical star configuration. Nodes are connected via the node cable to node ports which are, in turn, connected into the ring via relays in the wire centre. The logical topology, however, is still that of a ring. Each node receives data from the ring and passes data to the next node. Hence all nodes must repeat the signal to ensure the integrity of the data as it moves round the ring. This differs from the CSMA/CD (Ethernet) concept where only one node transmits and the signal is broadcast in all directions to every node.

We must be able to control nodes joining and leaving the ring (station access) to ensure that a new node, along with its node cable, cannot bring the ring 'down'.

The design rules will ensure that the ring infrastructure (size) is within the limits required to ensure good data is received by all nodes. They will also ensure that when new nodes join the ring, the node cable is within the limits so as to maintain this integrity.

Although the MAC frames are transparent to the user, the network design rules take into consideration how data is transmitted around the ring. Of the 25 or so MAC frames, we only need to consider those MAC frames or functions associated with:

- signal transmission and retiming, and
- joining and leaving the ring,

in order to understand why there are certain limits which are taken into consideration in the recommendations in later chapters.

For a more detailed list of MAC frames and guidance as to their use, please see the TMS 380 User Guide.

Signal transmission

The IEEE 802.5 network signal is Manchester encoded for transmission onto the ring cable with a maximum line clock rate of 8 MHz for the 4 Mbps Token Ring standard or 32 MHz for the 16 Mbps standard. The signal is regenerated (retimed and reclocked) by every attached node (host) active on the ring, but is only reset to the reference phase *once* round the ring. The node responsible for resetting the phase and controlling the reference clock on the ring is called the

active monitor. This node periodically generates an active monitor present MAC frame so that the remaining nodes (**standby monitors**) know that the ring clock is being managed.

Any node can become an active monitor, should the active monitor leave; the first node to join a ring will automatically become the active monitor.

Although the signal is regenerated by every active node, component tolerances, cable characteristics and transmission effects mean that the phase of the bitstream making up the signal data will not stay perfectly aligned with the reference phase of the active monitor. The amount of phase shift will depend on the number of nodes, the type and quality of cable, and the frequency of transmission. This phase shift is commonly known as **jitter**.

Jitter is important because if the phase shift becomes too great, at some point the Token Ring card in the next node will not be able to recover the timing from the incoming data stream and errors will result. A certain level of jitter can be compensated for by having buffer memory (known as elastic buffer) as part of the chipset. The elastic buffer on the active monitor card will reset the phase each time the data goes round the ring.

At 4 Mbps the elastic buffer is 30 bits (15 bauds), making it possible to compensate for the jitter equivalent of 260 nodes on IBM Type 1 quality cable.

When the transmission speed is increased to 16 Mbps, 126 bits (63 bauds) of elastic buffer are needed to compensate for the additional jitter built up as a result of the higher frequencies used.

The elastic buffer is used to monitor the ring for frequency errors in the rest of the adapters functioning in standby monitor mode.

The design rules take account of this jitter build-up by recommending the maximum number of nodes per ring depending on cable type and ring speed. They also take into consideration the signal **attenuation** which is proportional to the length of cable and number of wire centres. Each wire centre in the main ring will attenuate the signal by an amount equivalent to the wire centre loss, the level of which will also depend on whether the ring is running at 4 or 16 Mbps.

Joining and leaving the ring

A node wishing to join the ring must generate a join ring command to cause the relay in the wire centre to operate. However, we do not want the node to join the ring if, in doing so, it causes errors or adversely affects the operation of the ring. Therefore an adapter will

1

carry out three main tests when joining the ring, under MAC frame control, before it starts to transmit *live* data.

Lobe media test   Before the node (adapter) can join the ring, the lobe media test checks the continuity of the wire from the node to the wire centre. If the cable is not connected, or if there is a cable fault, or a node port fault on the wire centre, the node will not join the ring.

Speed test   On joining the ring, the adapter issues a claim token command frame to allow it to access the ring to carry out further initialization tests. If there is a speed mismatch all the cards see large timing errors, known as streaming. Once the ring has gone into streaming mode, the active monitor issues a ring purge causing all nodes to leave the ring momentarily (logically not physically) and the wrong-speed adapter to log the speed mismatch. Following the ring purge, all nodes return to the ring except the adapter that is set to the wrong speed.

Duplicate address test   Once 'in-ring' the node will first send a packet with the destination address as its own address. When it receives the packet back it checks the frame copied field, which should not be set because no other node should respond to this address. If it is set there is another node on the network with this address and this node will then leave the ring. All adapters have a unique Read Only Memory (ROM) node address known as a Burned In Address (BIA). However, software addresses can also be used, overriding the hardware address and possibly giving rise to a duplicate address condition. We must therefore ensure that, in our designs, all nodes and associated node cables enable the ring to continue to run free from errors as they join and leave the ring.

1.6   Errors and beaconing

As we have seen, all adapters monitor the ring for errors. Soft errors are those that can affect data but do not bring the ring down, and from which the ring quickly recovers. These are reported to the Ring Error Monitor (REM) which can be accessed by higher order software (typically the network manager) to monitor the status of the ring.

Hard errors are those that cause continuous data corruption or bring the ring down. In either case the MAC frame stability will be lost and/or the ring will not be able to transmit data. This status will be the result of a 'bad' cable, faulty card (adapter) or a physical break in the ring (which cannot be automatically isolated).

If this occurs, the adapter downstream from the fault or break will start to send **beacon** frames and the ring is said to be **beaconing**. This is an excellent way to isolate a fault quickly because the source address of the node is contained in the beacon frame. The management software, if it has sufficient functionality, can then identify where the beaconing node is situated and hence the approximate position of the fault.

1.7   Considerations for 16 Mbps network designs

The design rules and examples will show what node cable distances and main ring cable lengths can be supported for a given number of wire centres at both 4 and 16 Mbps operation. If, however, a network is initially going to run at 4 Mbps and then be upgraded to 16 Mbps, you must either design the network as if it were a 16 Mbps ring or be aware that you may have to modify the design later.

As we have seen, the **phase jitter** will increase in going from 4 to 16 Mbps and this will affect the cable lengths the ring will be able to support. The higher bit rate also demands higher quality cable to reduce attenuation and crosstalk. It is difficult to change cable lengths and even more so to replace the cable for one of a better quality when you upgrade the speed of your network, so forward planning is essential. We will look at these factors further as we go into the design in more detail in the following chapters.

In addition to speed and early token release, larger packet sizes are supported when running at 16 Mbps. The maximum packet size allowed at 4 Mbps is 4 Kbytes but at 16 Mbps it is 18 Kbytes. Whilst some applications can support these larger packet sizes, many cannot. It is advisable to check the operating system and application software if packet size is an important consideration in your overall network architecture. Packet size does not affect the physical design of Token

Ring networks, whereas the speed or bitrate is an important factor that we must take into consideration.

Now that we have seen (in principle) how token rings work let us look at the specific factors that determine how we design Token Ring networks.

2

Network planning overview

CHAPTER CONTENTS

Chapter summary

Having considered the principles on which a Token Ring network is based in Chapter 1 and had a brief introduction to the topology, we can now look at the wider aspects of the technology with respect to network planning.

Chapter 2 begins by considering the more general factors influencing designs including signal quality, the physical distance over which the network must work, design for maintenance and other environmental issues. It then goes on to discuss how these factors affect the major elements of the network, nodes and access units, and introduces the concepts of 'structured' and 'non structured' cabling systems to accommodate the varying environmental and physical (site) requirements.

This theme is then expanded as we look at the different types of media used in Token Ring designs and how they can be mixed on a single ring. Consideration is then given to larger networks in terms of the requirement to repeat the signal, thus introducing Token Ring **repeaters**. The differences between standalone and integrated repeaters is then discussed and related to how this will affect network planning.

Finally we introduce and outline the overall planning steps which will be more fully discussed in the following chapters.

2

2.1   Network design considerations

This chapter introduces the basic concepts of Token Ring network design and the seven planning steps. In the following chapters we will work through these seven steps with examples which will illustrate the inherent simplicity of Token Ring designs. The guidelines and recommendations we are going to consider will give the designer a set of rules which can then be used to accommodate variations in functionality and features from different Token Ring equipment manufacturers.

The goal of the network planner is to design a reliable network that will enable users to link together a number of computers, computer-based resources and/or computer-related systems. In order to do this the network planner should be aware of the key factors that will affect the design. These are:

- nodes and placement thereof
- access units (MAUs or wire centres)
- repeaters to regenerate the signal
- media
- environmental factors and
- costs.

Let us look at these factors in a little more detail and then summarize the stages in the design or planning steps.

2.2 Nodes

A node on a Token Ring network is defined as any device which has a unique node address and is capable of transmitting and receiving data packets to/from the ring. In order to connect a node to the ring, a network interface adapter card is required. This is often simply known as an interface, adapter, interface card or adapter card. The adapter is plugged into the computer or host node enabling it to be connected to the network. Different forms of adapter are required for different hosts and computers. Adapters are available for a wide range of IBM PC and MCA personal computers and clones, for Extended Industry Standard Architecture (EISA) machines, for many IBM host machines and for specified third party systems such as routers.

Adapter cards are either single board systems or mother board/ daughter board assemblies with edge connectors for the host **bus**. All adapters should have a 9-way, female, D-type connector for the Shielded Twisted Pair (STP) network cable to conform to the IEEE 802.5 specifications. Some interface adapters are also supplied with RJ45 connectors and on-board media filters for connection to **Unshielded Twisted Pair (UTP)** cable systems. A separate media filter with D-type to RJ conversion is available from several suppliers to connect adapters that do not have on-board media filter support.

Most non-IBM adapter cards utilize the Texas Instruments TMS 380 chipsets (although others are available), operating at 4 or 4/16 Mbps, which fully conform to the IEEE 802.5 Token Ring specifications and recommendations.

A single ring can support a maximum of 260 active nodes using shielded twisted pair (IBM Type 1) cable, in accordance with the IEEE 802.5 standard. This number depends on the level of signal distortion or 'jitter' built up as the data passes round the ring. As we saw earlier, jitter levels are a function of the number of nodes, the type of cable and the data rate. Jitter increases as more active nodes join the ring; if more than 260 nodes are active on a single ring, data errors may occur. This is not usually a restriction as most LANs limit the maximum number of nodes to a hundred or less for reasons of management and performance.

Node independent networks

The majority of networks operating at 4/16 Mbits/s will be designed to enable nodes to join or leave the ring at any time without affecting overall network operation. To achieve this, the network must be designed so that any active node, anywhere in the network, can drive a signal reliably around the whole network and back to itself. This is essential because we do not know what combination of nodes will be in the ring at any one time and hence where the active nodes will be.

2

The planning rules have been formulated to enable any single active node in the ring to send a message round the whole ring and back to itself. This results in a network that can be sustained by any node, anywhere on the ring, and is thus independent of a particular node or group of nodes being active to work correctly. The purpose of the designer, therefore, is to plan the network so that it is independent of which nodes are on; the design is then said to be **node independent**.

It is possible to modify the node independent design by assuming that file servers are on at all times when the network has to be available and that these can be relied upon to regenerate the signal. TAKE CARE if only one node is a dependent node; if it is removed (or leaves), the network could fail. This is quite possible in a multi-file-server configuration and hence is not recommended.

In planning Token Ring networks, then, we are planning for node independent networks.

2.3 Multistation access units

As we saw in Chapter 1, the multistation access unit (MAU), or wire centre, is the heart of the Token Ring network and is designed to protect the integrity of the network by ensuring that ring continuity is maintained irrespective of the state of the attached hosts. The MAUs and interconnections from ring-out to ring-in ports form the physical ring configuration. Nodes are connected to **lobe** ports on the MAU via directly attached cable or through distribution panels and wall plates in a permanently wired system. See Figure 2.1.

All Token Ring MAUs should be designed to comply with the IEEE 802.5 specifications. Each wire centre (MAU) typically connects

(a) Structured cabling scheme

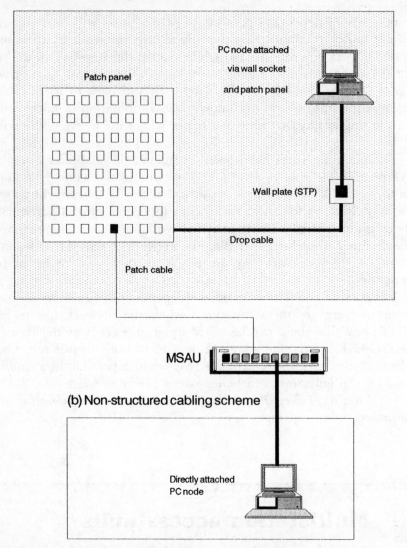

(b) Non-structured cabling scheme

Figure 2.1 Methods of connecting nodes to access units: (a) Structured cabling scheme. This type of system normally has wiring closets for the wire centres and associated racks. Patch panels are used to terminate the building cables from workgroup areas and wall plates in offices. (b) Non-structured cabling scheme. These typically connect nodes directly to wire centres for smaller workgroups and less permanent installations.

up to eight nodes, although both smaller and larger capacity MAUs are now available. When a node wants to join the ring, line current from the host is used to operate the associated relay at the lobe port of the MAU. Expansion beyond eight nodes is accomplished by linking together two or more MAUs to give the required capacity. MAUs are connected together by ring-in (RI) and ring-out (RO) expansion ports. The ring-out of one MAU is connected to the ring-in of the next and the last wire centre is connected back to the first in the same way to realize a closed ring system.

2

An alternative method of providing greater connectivity is to use a **wiring concentrator**. The concentrator is designed as a standard 19 inch rack mount chassis which supports modular, multiport lobe media cards. Up to 10 or 20 ports can be configured on a single card and, depending on the size of cards and chassis, a single wiring concentrator can provide the connectivity for 40, 80 or even 160 nodes. If wiring concentrators are chosen to provide node access, as opposed to separate 8-node MAUs, then the initial cost associated with the chassis, power supplies and control modules must be considered.

Lobe media cards are available for STP, UTP and fibre optic connections, depending on the manufacturer. Some concentrators also provide *hot-swap* capability (exchanging modules with the power supply on), dual redundant power supplies and network management capability.

Expansion beyond a single concentrator is via the ring-in and ring-out ports in the same way as for the equivalent 8-node MAU. Concentrators are available with a single ring-in and ring-out port and, in some cases, with plug-in cards that provide ring in/out ports and can also support the common media options STP, UTP and fibre, lobe ports.

Wiring concentrators and 8-node MAUs can be mixed on the same ring according to the recommendations of the respective manufacturers and suppliers.

Managing the ring(s) infrastructure

Some manufacturers have extended the basic connection functions of the wire centres by adding maintenance and control features to improve the availability of the network. Node isolation switches and Light Emitting Diode (LED) status indicators on node ports, ring-in and ring-out ports show which are active and enable system managers to isolate any part of the ring without having physically to disconnect cables. MAUs with in-built intelligence, usually accessed via a secondary, low-speed serial bus, are also available. They enable wire centres (and hence the cable infrastructure) to be controlled from a central management station.

Wiring concentrators normally include some form of network management at the physical level because a fault on a concentrator could result in all nodes being removed from the ring, as opposed to a maximum of eight nodes in the event of an 8-node MAU becoming faulty.

Access for and control of these additional management features can be either via the network itself (in-band), by a separate management network (out-band) or by a combination of the two. In-band systems can only manage the rings if the rings are working, while out-band systems will not have access to ring statistics and media access control (MAC) frame information. A management system that uses in-band and out-band control is most effective and can even isolate wire centres, cables and nodes if the ring is down. This will realize the highest availability and the minimum time to isolate faults.

Networks should be designed, wherever possible, to facilitate network maintenance and fault-finding. Simple linear topologies are easier to maintain than complex hierarchical ones. The designer should plan to meet the requirements with the minimum level of complexity.

2.4   Network repeaters

Token Ring topology does not impose any limitations on the maximum distance over which data can be transmitted except that resulting from signal attenuation which is a function of the medium used. Network size can be extended beyond the attenuation limits of the cable by using repeaters to regenerate the signals. It is necessary to repeat or regenerate the signal, other than at an active node, when the number of wire centres or the length of cable in the ring would introduce an unacceptable level of attenuation.

The task of the designer is to recognize when a network requires repeaters and then to decide where they have to be placed. Repeaters will normally only be required on relatively large rings. Remember that they are used to ensure that the network will function correctly irrespective of when and where nodes are attached.

The repeater can be regarded as a node that never intercepts packets but passes them all on, regenerating the signal in the same way that an attached node would do. In fact, electronically this is exactly what the repeater does and so it also introduces jitter in the signal. Thus whenever networks are designed with repeaters, the maximum number of attached nodes has to be reduced by the number of repeaters in the network.

(This would only be a limitation on a network with almost 260 users connected over a large area where several repeaters may have to be used.)

As mentioned briefly in Chapter 1, as the signal passes through each active node or repeater a slight phase shift is introduced. This phase shift, or jitter, accumulates with each node and has to be corrected in order to extract reliable timing information. A shift register in each adapter repeater enables the circuits to accommodate this phase shift by moving the bit stream in relation to the derived clock. There is a limit to the number of times this correction can be applied when the signal is only reclocked once round the ring; for IEEE 802.5 compatible networks this is equivalent to a maximum of 260 active nodes (at 4 Mbps). Note: although IEEE 802.5 adapters have a 48-bit node address capability, the practical limit of 260 nodes as the maximum that can be connected to a single ring is a function of the accumulated jitter and not the addressing range. In practice this is not a serious limitation because single rings are usually kept well below 200 nodes (typically 50 to 100) for ease of management. Large networks are designed as multiple rings linked by **bridges, routers** or file servers.

Repeaters are available as standalone units (which can be rack mounted) or as integral units within the wire centre (MAU), depending on the manufacturer. Network designs based on wire centres with integral repeaters reduce the amount of cabling required, are easier to design and, as there is less equipment, are generally more reliable than designs based on standalone repeaters. See Figure 2.2.

Fibre optic cable introduces less attenuation than copper cable making it possible to achieve distances up to 3 km between fibre optic repeaters.

2.5 Media considerations

Token Ring networks can run over different types of media, including shielded twisted pair copper cable, unshielded twisted pair copper cable and optical fibre. The IEEE 802.5 specification currently supports the **IBM structured cabling system** based on Type 1 copper

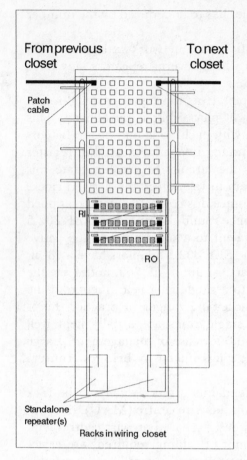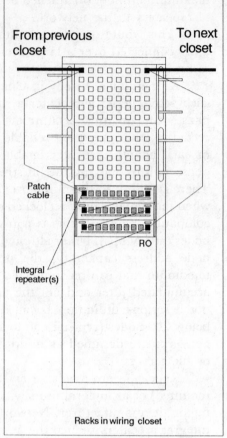

RI : Ring-in
RO : Ring-out

Figure 2.2 Standalone and integral repeater configurations showing how the cables are connected – not how they should be routed. Repeaters are used to extend the physical size of the network. They can be either standalone or integral with the wire centre or hub.

cable and optical fibre. The AT&T **Premises Distribution System (PDS)**, which is based on telephone-type, data grade copper cable, uses level 3, level 4, and level 5 classification categories (e.g. **DIW**-24/4, **AWG**-24 or **Systimax**™ 1061/2061 respectively). See Appendix A for further details on media.

In many buildings cables will have to be run in conduits, possibly giving rise to different cable lengths than shown on a point-to-point drawing. Care should be taken to ensure all cable lengths used in designing networks reflect the actual cable run on the associated drawings.

In some cases existing conduits may be full, limiting the number of new cables that can be installed. In these cases it may be more cost-effective to install fibre optic cables in existing conduits than to install new conduits.

2

2.6   Environmental factors

The proposed LAN environment can directly affect the choice of medium. STP data grade cabling is specifically designed for high speed, digital data networks and is used to achieve a greater distance between repeaters and a higher noise immunity than UTP cabling, although at a higher cost. UTP cabling, often referred to as 'tele-phone-type' cable, can be used quite effectively in low noise environments over short distances, typically 100 metres.

UTP cable usually costs less than STP cable and optical fibre, and is more flexible than the equivalent STP cable. For these reasons it is becoming an increasingly popular choice for LANs running at up to 20 Mbps.

Fibre optic cable should be considered for high noise environments, where data security is important, and for all external runs where electrical surges are quite common (e.g. between buildings). Fireproof or fire-resistant cable may have to be used depending on the application and local fire regulations. Ensure that any environmental factors that could affect your LAN design have been considered.

2.7   Costs

Networks can be designed in a variety of ways depending on the site requirements, customer requirements and the preferences of the designer. Networks should be planned to give the best in terms of satisfying these requirements at the most economical cost. It is possible to get a good appreciation of the cost-effectiveness of any design by working out the capital cost per node of the proposed network and comparing it with previous examples.

2.8 Planning stages

Before implementing any network design, a network plan should be developed. The plan should be a step-by-step list of everything that has to be done to design, procure, install, commission and maintain a Token Ring LAN in a building or group of buildings.

One basis for a network plan is to consider the proposed data loading factors and position resources (file servers, printers) accordingly. In a single ring design, file and communication servers are often sited in the same room as equipment racks or in separate (usually adjacent) computer rooms, for security reasons. Print servers can be sited centrally and/or near workgroups for easier access. In terms of ring design these are all nodes and should be sited to satisfy user requirements whilst conforming to the respective design rules.

In larger installations traffic can be managed better by splitting the system into several smaller rings. In these designs the commonly used resources should be available on a per-ring basis (cost permitting) so as to minimize inter-ring traffic. A central file server (or servers) can then be used where a single, central database or program store is required. Additional shared resources (e.g. communications gateways) can be sited so as to provide the most convenient access while still considering the effect on inter-ring traffic and user response times.

The decision to adopt a multiple ring design and where to place the rings will depend very much on the type of application, customer requirements and cost factors not covered in this book, which is intended to introduce a method of designing and planning Token Rings by looking at the considerations for a single ring network. Once the single ring has been designed, multiple ring networks can be designed by linking rings by bridges, routers or gateways, remembering that these devices are simply nodes on each of their respective rings and treating them accordingly in the design.

Token Ring networks can be designed by siting wire centres in or near workgroups or in centralized **wiring closets** (communications rooms with racks to mount wire centres and ancillary equipment) as used in telephone installation practice.

Network planning and implementation time will be related directly to the size of the ring which, in turn, will depend on the number of nodes, wire centres and wiring closets.

The size of the ring will also dictate whether a single wiring closet, multiple wiring closets or multiple wiring closets with repeaters design is necessary. Larger rings will take longer to design and install than smaller rings and will almost certainly have to be planned and installed in phases.

2

The following list summarizes the planning steps to follow in designing a Token Ring network:

(1) Determine the location of present and (if possible) future nodes from user requirements and supplier recommendations.

(2) Determine the location of wiring closets and wire centres from site details, user requirements and desired topology.

(3) Determine media requirements from site details, environmental factors, network size and topology.

(4) Determine repeater requirements from network size and topology.

(5) Verify network design: ensure design is node independent and conforms to recommendations.

(6) Perform cost analysis: calculate approximate per node cost on capital costs only.

(7) Finalize network plan: check all changes, verify as good design and certify.

In the next chapter we begin designing Token Rings by implementing the first step – positioning the nodes.

3

Defining and locating nodes

CHAPTER CONTENTS

Chapter summary

In order to design a LAN, the network planner goes through an iterative process of positioning the nodes, wiring closets and associated equipment according to where the customer wants them and then comparing this with the design rules and criteria for the particular technology and equipment being used. If the placement of nodes breaks any of the rules (e.g. distance between them, maximum number per LAN **segment**), then the designer must amend the plans to try to conform to the rules (in order for the network to run) whilst still trying to meet the requirement. To achieve this the designer might have to take recommendations back to the customer so that he can, if necessary, change the layout.

In this chapter we look at the first part of the design process, that of positioning the nodes. In the next chapter we will look at the second part of the process, that of deciding where to place the wiring centres and associated equipment, such as **patch panels** and repeaters. We will also look at Token Ring topology in relation to the interconnection of the wiring centres.

In the following chapters we will introduce and discuss the third and subsequent parts of the process, the design rules. The design rules are outlined for networks based on shielded and unshielded twisted pair cable and fibre optic cable as these are the three main types of media used on Token Ring LANs today.

In order to be able to decide where to place nodes and wire centres you will need relevant site information, including drawings. In addition, planning forms should be used to assist in the design, making the whole process as straightforward and reliable as possible. These are discussed in this chapter together with an example of a typical equipment list, or schedule, for the LAN components.

Finally, so that you can begin to apply these (possibly new) concepts in a practical way, we take an example – called the 'sample office layout' – which we will use in the rest of this book to illustrate the design planning, and verification stages.

The more familiar you become with Token Ring design and the more networks you plan, the quicker and easier the process becomes. Whilst it takes time to explain, especially if the concepts are new, it is soon easy to do. Several examples are included as we move on to the design rules proper which illustrate how the rules can be applied quickly to verify a network design. Rough designs can be checked before the detailed planning gets underway and preliminary plans can be altered easily to ensure conformity with the user requirements and design rules. Within a short time you will begin to place nodes, and wiring centres, so that the design rules are satisfied from the outset, further reducing the time taken in the design stages.

3.1   Beginning the design

Now that we have an outline plan to follow we can move on to the next stage and see what we now need to do to design a structured Token Ring network.

(If we were only interested in getting a rough idea of the feasibility of a design or if a non-structured network would suffice, then not all of the details mentioned below would be necessary. We could do a first pass by knowing how many nodes are required, the ring speed and the type of cable preferred. Indeed, dashing off a quick estimate like this for feasibility is often done by the network planner to get a feel for the network before starting the full design.)

We have seen that the suggested planning steps are:

(1)   Determine the location of present and future nodes.

(2)   Determine the location of wiring closets and wire centres.

(3)   Determine the media requirements.

(4)   Determine the repeater requirements.

(5)   Verify the network design.

(6)   Perform the cost analysis.

(7)   Finalize the network plan.

In this chapter we look at the first step – how to position the nodes. To do this we will need certain documentation and, not as critical but still important, will need to know what types of nodes to expect.

Let us first consider the documentation requirements, then look briefly at the main types of nodes and, finally, take a typical office (the sample office layout) and use this as an example for this section and the remaining steps in our network design.

3.2   Documentation

To design our structured network we will need:

- Building blueprints: Copies of all relevant building drawings schematics and scaled layouts of the proposed site where the network is to be installed. These will be used to determine the exact locations of nodes in relation to internal walls and partitions, conduits and communications rooms. Drawings must contain distance information, the exact dimensions of rooms, the distances between rooms and the ceiling heights. When using this data to determine cable lengths, ensure that cable drops and/or rises are included. Drawings should also show access points and any preferred or non-preferred routing for cables, particularly floor-to-floor wiring runs for multi-level installations.

- Detailed layouts: It is important to know the exact locations and dimensions of modular walls and furniture when cable has to run through or round it and when nodes are sited in these areas. In temporary installations and offices where nodes are frequently moved, ensure that any changes to distance calculations do not contravene the planning rules outlined in later chapters.

3

Many manufacturers make workgroup (or satellite) wire centres. These simplify network design and reduce cabling and maintenance costs. They are particularly suitable for expanding the number of nodes that can be supported at a location without having to run multiple cables back to the wiring closet or redesigning the network. They are also useful where temporary nodes are required or in installations where nodes are moved frequently. These wire centres are often located at or near the workgroup nodes, hence the term **'workgroup' wire centres**.

If workgroup wire centres are an option, they should be considered at this stage in the design, depending on the application and site requirements. These requirements will dictate whether workgroup wire centres are incorporated as part of the main design or added later to accommodate growth and network changes.

Network design forms

Although you can design networks without forms, we have found that having the correct documentation is invaluable for any type of network. Consequently, to assist in planning the network a series of network design forms has been included for you to use. They are the equipment schedule(s), cable schedule(s), rack chart(s) and sequence chart(s). Examples of the types of form that can be used are included in Appendix C. They may be copied, if you wish, to enable you to document your network.

These are not the only forms that can be used. Network designers may have a preference for their own forms and lists and, provided they adequately cover the details required, they should be fine.

In addition to these forms, network schematics, block diagrams and any other information required to make the overall design and maintenance of the network easier and more reliable should be prepared.

Typically the forms will provide the following information:

- Equipment schedules: Used to keep a running list of the components and parts selected during planning the network. When the network design is finished, the equipment schedule(s) will show the adapter cards, wire centres, repeaters and media required for your network. An approximate value for the cost per node can thus be found and an equipment ordering schedule prepared.

- Cable schedule: Similar to a spreadsheet, this schedule should include information on every cable in the network by name, location and (most importantly) length. Additional information to make identification and maintenance easier may include the node address (where applicable), the cable number or identification, and where the cable goes from and to. The nearest telephone number to the cable run is also very useful during installation and maintenance. Where systems have to be installed over existing cable, you should ensure that all necessary information is available to enable you to design the network. If the installation is subcontracted, then ensure that the subcontractor fully completes the cable schedules or that they provide similar schedules themselves to enable you to design the network.

- Rack charts: Used to identify the position of all wiring closets (wiring closet schedule) and racks/wire centres (MAUs) within closets (rack layouts). Copy and fill in as many forms as necessary to cover the network completely. It is often useful, and will help to complete and check the forms, to produce a sketch of the overall network. This can then be used to place wiring closets and racks and to check inter-rack and inter-closet cabling. Forms should be completed with the numbering scheme you have chosen for your design. A suggested numbering scheme is shown in the examples in Chapter 4. You can use your own numbering system so long as it uniquely and clearly identifies closets and racks within closets.

- Sequence charts: Contain information on the sequence of connections between wire centres. We have shown two types:
  - Wire centre sequence chart, for connections between standard wire centres, hubs or concentrators.
  - Workgroup wire centre sequence chart, for connections between workgroup (or satellite) wire centres and their associated 'parent' hub.

These charts should be used to show wire centre numbers and connections to adjacent wire centres. The sequence charts also include the length of the longest node cable (or **lobe length**) for every wire centre. This information will be used later when we determine what the **Maximum Lobe Length** (MLL) for a given configuration will be.

3

3.3   Types of node

Each Token Ring host requires an interface board to connect it to the network. This is often referred to as an adapter, adapter card or network interface card (NIC). The type of interface will depend on the bus structure of the host computer. Interface cards normally connect to STP or UTP copper cable, although they can also be connected to fibre optic cable if a suitable fibre converter is available.

As a result of the wide range of host computer systems available, different interfaces are required to connect them to an IEEE 802.5 Token Ring. In most cases they will be supplied by the computer manufacturer. As IBM have adopted the IEEE 802.5 Token Ring as one of their preferred network standards, they offer direct host connectivity for several of their own computer systems. Other common hosts include PCs, bridges/routers and gateways.

Let us now look briefly at these main types of node as we mark them on our site layouts.

PC nodes

Token Ring PC interfaces are available from several independent vendors for Industry Standard Architecture (ISA), Extended Industry Standard Architecture (EISA) and Microchannel Architecture (MCA) systems.

When equipped with the relevant card, any personal computer that is both hardware and software compatible with an IBM PC, XT, AT(ISA), EISA or MCA machine can be used as a node on a Token Ring network. Non-IBM ISA and MCA-based products as well as EISA products are usually designed to comply with the IBM (ISA) and EISA specifications in terms of bus speed and bus timing. IBM and EISA computers that comply with these specifications can support a wide range of interfaces from different manufacturers and will run on the same ring as systems with IBM cards.

Compatibility with the IBM Token Ring is achieved by using the IBM **TROPIC** chipset on the interface card or by providing a compatible (software) interface at level 2, the **data link layer**, of the **Open Systems Interconnection (OSI)** model. The latter is achieved by having specific operating system driver software for each type of card. These 'drivers', as they are known, are normally supplied by the card manufacturer or the operating system vendor.

A standard data link layer interface has been adopted by the IEEE; known as the IEEE 802.2 **Logical Link Control (LLC)** standard, it provides a common interface to the higher layers of software as defined in the OSI seven-layer model.

Adapters with IEEE 802.2 support can be freely mixed on the same ring to run applications that use the IEEE 802.2 standard. Many IBM PC-based applications adopt this standard and can thus be run with third-party adapters and IEEE 802.2 LLC code. In addition, many other software products include IEEE 802.2 support (e.g. TCP/IP) and can thus be used in a mixed vendor Token Ring environment. See Figure 3.1.

Applications that do not use IEEE 802.2 can also run over a wide range of different cards if drivers are available for the card and associated software. These native drivers, as they are called, almost always provide better performance and often better functionality than IEEE 802.2 drivers because they can be optimized for the card type and operating system software.

In an attempt to provide a standard interface without loss of performance and to offer enhanced functions (e.g. multiple protocols on the same card), some software vendors have developed common data link interfaces of their own and encouraged card manufacturers to adopt them.

The two most well known and widely used standards in this category are the **Open Data Link Interface** (OD(L)I), which is used by Novell in their NetWare operating system and the **Network Device Interface Support (NDIS)** from Microsoft which is used in the **LAN Manager** operating system. IBM also include support for NDIS in their **OS/2** operating system software products.

For PCs that do not have a local disk (i.e. diskless workstations), interfaces can be fitted with a boot PROM which enables the workstation to be booted directly from the file server over the network and controls the loading of the operating system and workstation shell software.

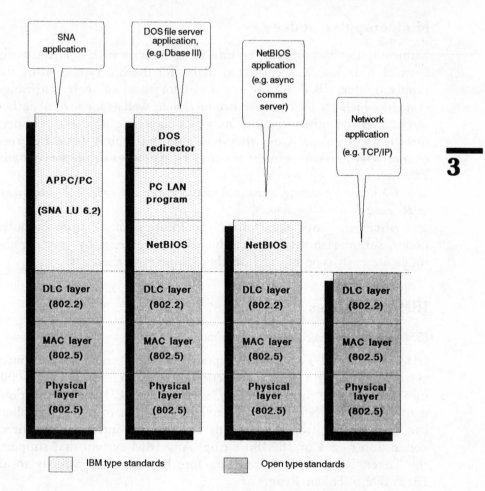

Figure 3.1 Standards interface for Token Ring adapters. Compatibility with IBM Token Ring adapters and software is achieved with a common software interface at level 2 of the OSI model (data link layer). ODI and NDIS drivers offer additional standard interfaces.

For network planning, mark each personal computer host node on the site layouts at the exact location required.

After you have determined the location of all personal computer nodes, you can summarize the interface board requirements, and boot ROMs for diskless PCs, by entering the totals for each type of card/ROM on the equipment schedules.

Minicomputer nodes

Minicomputer systems can be interfaced directly with a Token Ring network if an interface card is available for the bus type used by the minicomputer. IBM supply interfaces for most of their mid-range systems which are currently in production as well as for several earlier models. While other vendors may not have the ability to connect directly to a Token Ring, they will almost certainly have Ethernet connectivity and can connect via routers, gateways or file servers and Ethernet.

For network planning, mark each minicomputer host node on the site layouts at the exact location required.

After you have determined the location of all minicomputer nodes, summarize the interface board requirements by entering the totals for each type of card on the equipment schedules.

IBM host nodes

IBM mainframe/minicomputer connections

IBM provide full Token Ring support for a wide range of computer systems via either a direct connection (system/36, AS/400, RS/6000) or a Front End Processor (FEP), such as the 3174 communications controller and 37X5 cluster controllers. Versions of these controllers can be supplied (from IBM) with Token Ring interfaces for direct connection to a 4 or 16 Mbit/s ring. Any IBM system that supports the Token Ring network can therefore be connected directly to an IEEE 802.5 Token Ring.

The IEEE 802.2 interface and its associated adapter software enables users to run standard IBM communications software (LAN support program, personal communications software, APPC/PC, etc.) over non-IBM cards and connect to IBM machines. For example, the PC version of IBM's peer-to-peer protocols Applications Peer-to-Peer Communication (APPC) supports the IEEE 802.2 standard.

For network planning, mark each IBM host attachment on the site layouts at the exact location required.

After you have determined the location of all IBM host nodes, summarize the interface board requirements by entering the totals for each type of card on the equipment schedules.

SNA gateways

Of the many ways of connecting into an IBM system via an SNA gateway, the two most common are discussed below.

In an IBM communications LAN environment a non-dedicated gateway PC is used to connect to external systems that may not have direct Token Ring support. Non-IBM interface cards can be used and mixed freely with IBM cards in these networks except for the gateway PC. This usually requires an IBM adapter if it uses IBM proprietary software (and hence microcode) or a specific third-party adapter if it is running third-party software (and hence microcode).

For users running other communications software, Systems Network Architecture (SNA) gateway connections are normally provided as part of the networking package (usually optional). A synchronous interface is fitted into the file server or a non-dedicated PC and is then connected to the IBM 37X5 cluster controller either locally or over a remote modem link.

Whichever method is chosen, personal computers can log on to the mainframe (once the gateway PC has established the link) and have transparent terminal access and, in some cases, file transfer facilities.

For network planning, mark each SNA gateway node on the site layouts at the exact location required.

After you have determined the locations of all the SNA gateway nodes, summarize the interface board requirements by entering the totals for each type of card on the equipment schedules.

File servers

File servers based on personal computers will have been included in the equipment schedule totals, and should have been marked on the layouts when the personal computer nodes were placed. Other, dedicated file servers may also have to be connected to the ring. Direct Token Ring access is currently available for all major platforms, including those supplied by Novell, 3-COM, Banyan and Compaq file servers. Allow one interface per file server unless a multiple ring topology is being designed and file servers are intended to be used as routers, in which case create a separate equipment schedule for each ring.

For network planning, mark each file server node not already included on the site layouts at the exact location required.

After you have determined the locations of all file server nodes, summarize the interface board requirements by entering the totals for each type of card on the equipment schedules.

Bridge and router nodes

Separate and independent LANs can be connected together using bridges and routers. It is also possible to have a bridge and router in one unit; this is called a **bridging router** or **brouter**. For network planning purposes, bridges, routers and bridging routers can be considered as similar products.

Note that bridges are ISO layer 2 network extension products which are transparent to layer 3 **protocols** and above in accordance with the ISO 7-layer model. They use bridge control protocols to manage the passage of data through the bridged networks. One standard for managing bridged Ethernets is the **Spanning Tree Bridging** (STB) protocol, while **Source Routing Bridging protocol** (SRB) is used for managing bridged Token Rings. A further protocol type, known as Source Routing Transparent (SRT), is required to bridge a mixture of interconnected Ethernets and Token Rings.

Note also that routers are ISO layer 3 routing devices which can interconnect different physical LANs and provide higher levels of functionality than bridges. File servers with connections to two or more networks (multiple cards in the file server) are often said to be providing a 'bridge' between the networks attached to the file server. However, in almost all cases the file server will actually route packets between networks and therefore behaves as a router, not a bridge.

Bridges, bridging routers and routers also support wide area network (WAN) connections via leased lines, **ISDN**, **frame relay**, **asynchronous transfer mode** (ATM) and X25 packet switched systems.

A bridge or router will appear as a node on the Token Ring network and as a node on any other network to which it is attached. Networks to which bridge/router(s) may be connected include IEEE 802.5 Token Ring, Apollo Token Ring, **Fibre Distributed Data Interface** (FDDI) Token Ring, Ethernet version 1.0, 2.0 and IEEE 802.3, serial lines, ISDN frame relay, ATM and X.25 circuits.

For network planning, mark each bridge/router node on the site layouts at the exact location required.

After you have determined the locations of all bridges, routers and/or bridging router nodes, summarize the interface board requirements by entering the totals for each type of card on the equipment schedules.

3.4   Stage one - summary

We should now have the required documentation for the installation we are planning and should have started to fill in the site layout and equipment schedules as follows:

- Site layouts: The layouts should now have all the nodes marked in their intended locations.
- Equipment schedules: The equipment schedule(s) should have the section on interface cards completed.

3

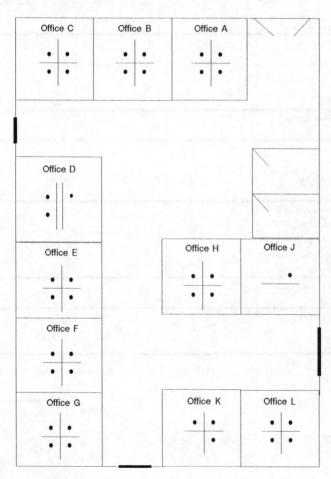

- PC nodes (39)

Figure 3.2   Sample office layout: placement of nodes. The nodes can be positioned from a schematic of the office layout, and instructions for placing PCs on desks, etc.

Equipment schedule

Designer [   ]   **Date** [   ]

Network no. [   ]   **Page no.** [   ] of [   ]

Item	Part no.	Quantity	Price
PC-bus I/F			
PC/AT-bus I/F		39	
MCA I/F			
EISA-bus I/F			
Boot ROMs			
Wire centres			
Power supply			
Power supply			
19" racks		2	
Data cable STP			
Data cable UTP			
Patch cables (3 m)			
Patch cables (10 m)			
Adapter cables		39	
Fibre optic cable			
Other items 1			
Other items 2			
		Total	

Figure 3.3 Example equipment schedule.

Design hints

Future nodes

If possible, the layout should be evaluated, in conjunction with the customer, for future expansion needs. It is often more cost-effective to plan and install network cabling, connectors, wall plates etc., sufficient to accommodate growth for between two and five years (depending on the application) than to have to redesign and perhaps change the network at a later date.

3

Fibre cabling

On installations using fibre optic cables, it is advisable to increase the capacity of the fibre optic cable pairs by two or three times that required for the initial installation. It will be more cost-effective to plan for future growth at the outset when the major plant costs are related to installation costs and will not vary a great deal as a result of the number of pairs in the fibre cable.

Site log

For ease of maintenance and to track the additions, moves and changes experienced by all network users, we recommend that a 'site log' be created. This should include details of the network configuration, designs, site drawings, contact names and telephone numbers, together with a summary of the maintenance history of the network. The site log should be created as soon as the network design has passed the preliminary feasibility stages and the requirement for a network has been confirmed. The log can then begin to capture information from the various design phases.

We close this chapter by providing a sample office layout (Figure 3.2) and a typical equipment schedule (Figure 3.3). We will continue to update these as we move on to the next phases of the design, steps 2, 3 and 4.

4

Wire closets, hubs and repeaters

CHAPTER CONTENTS

Chapter summary

Having looked at the placement of nodes as the first part of the design process, we can now position the wire centres and their associated wiring closets.

In this chapter we see how the logical ring network described in Chapter 1 becomes a physical star network of nodes (if they are connected to a single central wiring closet), or a distributed group of stars (if they are connected to several wiring closets linked via a **backbone** cable). In both cases the data is still passed from active node to active node maintaining the logical ring.

The chapter also includes a brief explanation of the common functions of the many different types of wire centre – wiring concentrators, multistation access units, hubs, hub concentrators and/or intelligent hubs. Although there are a variety of names, their common function is to act as the attachment point for the node cables. They only differ in terms of capacity, media support and management capabilities.

The requirements for Token Ring repeaters are then discussed both in terms of their ability to extend the physical size of the network (without reducing the distances from the node to the wire centres) and how they affect the design. The additional components that are necessary to make up the complete cabling system, including connector types, communication racks, distribution panels, **patch cables** and **adapter cables** are introduced; further details are included in Appendix A.

Having looked at the key infrastructure components – the physical building blocks that make up the ring – we can now see how they fit together: wire centres mounted in racks, racks sited in wiring closets and then the interconnections between them.

4

Good designs will provide sufficient connections to workstations, server nodes etc., as cost-effectively as possible. To do this the designer must balance the costs of cables from wiring closets to nodes (**lobe cables**) with the costs of provisioning wiring closets and racks. Therefore, we next consider the placement of wiring closets, using the sample office layout as a worked example. The various forms that can be used to help with the design are illustrated, partly completed to show the placement of wire centres within racks and wiring closets within the office.

Finally we return to a consideration of the maximum lobe length (MLL) – the longest length of cable from the wiring closet to the wall plate in the work area – which is usually the single most important factor or variable that the user needs to know and for which the designer must plan.

In later chapters we will introduce design formulae for calculating the MLL. We will show how to design networks based on STP and UTP copper cable and multimode fibre cable by considering three main ring topologies and the enhancements possible by using workgroup wire centres, when available.

4.1   Physical network

Having positioned the nodes in our network, we can now consider where the wire centres (hubs) and corresponding wiring closets (communications rooms) should go. In some cases the wiring closets may already exist. The network planner will then have to do some preliminary calculations (using the formulae described later) to decide whether or not the closets are in convenient locations. If they are then we can proceed with the design. If not, new closets may have to be proposed or the existing closets resited.

We then have to choose a physical topology to suit the customer's application and the network environment, for existing or new closets. For example, do we propose a single closet for our wire centres and connect all nodes in a single star formation or do we have two (or more) closets – linked by copper cable – and nodes connected via the nearest closet? If we have two or more closets, should they be linked together by fibre optic cable? See Figure 4.1.

In most installations, the application and costs will quickly decide what form the physical network will take, so this will not be the open-ended choice it might at first appear.

We can now move on to stages 2, 3 and 4 in our design. As a reminder, they are:

(2) Determining the location of wiring closets and wire centres.

(3) Determining the media.

(4) Determining the repeater requirements.

We have to look at these next steps together, though not necessarily in strict order, because each one affects the others. The designer will position closets and then, depending on the type of cable and the distances to the nodes, decide whether or not repeaters will be needed or whether to choose different locations for the closets. Each cycle involves verifying the design to check that the network will work. As the designer becomes more proficient, it will often be possible to position closets and decide whether repeaters will be needed in a single design iteration.

The final plan should take the following factors into consideration:

- existing site requirements
- customer requirements
- network requirements
- application
- budget.

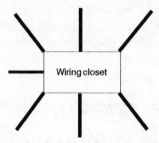

(a) Single wiring closet

4

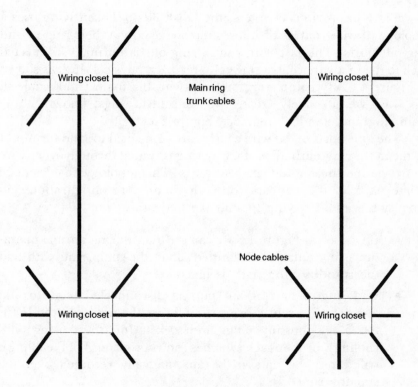

(b) Multiple wiring closet

Figure 4.1   Physical network topologies. (a) All nodes connected to a single wiring closet, and (b) Nodes connected to the nearest wiring closet in a multi-closet network.

In order to continue, we must ensure that we are familiar with the main components that make up the physical Token Ring: racks, wire centres, repeaters ... and the cable! We must also know how they fit together to form the backbone of a Token Ring. We therefore consider these next. Then we can address the above requirements in relation to the planning process, using the sample office layout as our example, to show how they give rise to the physical network.

4.2   Network components

Wire centres (hubs): interconnection

As we saw in previous chapters, the IEEE 802.5 Token Ring uses a topology of wire centres or hubs interconnected via their ring-in and ring-out ports. The last wire centre ring-out is normally connected back to the first wire centre ring-in to realize a physical ring, as shown in Figure 4.2. By completing the ring with the main trunk cable in this way, we effectively create two concentric rings, known as the main ring and standby ring. See Figure 4.3.

The lobe ports of the wire centres are connected to, and form part of, the **main ring path**. The standby ring is routed through every wire centre via the ring-in and ring-out ports. This topology enables us to isolate parts of the network for fault finding, reconfiguration and expansion without having to shut the network down:

- If we look at Figure 4.3 we can see that, during normal operation, ring data is transmitted along the main ring path and the **standby ring path** is inactive.

- If a ring-in or ring-out port is disconnected (e.g. to add another wire centre or to reconfigure the network) the IEEE 802.5 self-shorting plugs and sockets (on rings using STP cabling), or loopback switches (on rings using UTP cabling), will cause the data to be automatically rerouted over the standby ring.

- Ring continuity has been maintained and the standby ring is now also carrying data traffic.

Take care! If two such cables are removed from the ring then the network will partition into two separate rings; although both rings will continue to function, some users may lose access to key resources, such as file servers.

Note that the IEEE 802.5 connector used on STP networks (**Media Interface Connector**) loops the transmit data to the receive data when it is disconnected from the wire centre. This enables a cable

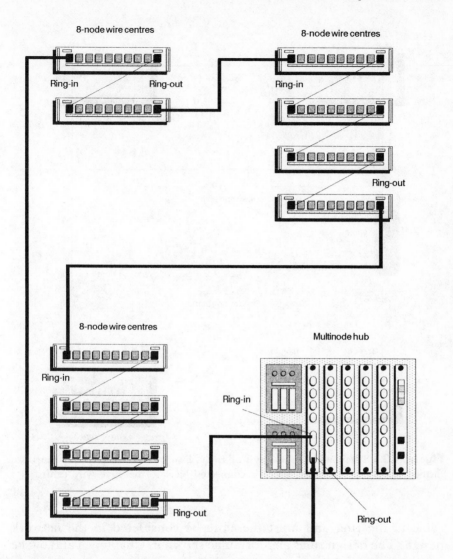

Figure 4.2 Wire centre (MAU) and concentrator (hub) connection. The wire centres and hubs are cabled together using ring-in/ring-out ports to realize the physical ring.

to be removed from anywhere in the network without opening the ring because the signal is looped back at the open socket created at each end of the break, thereby maintaining the overall ring circuit. The same loopback capability is also provided on some UTP wire centres (MAUs) via switches on the ring-in and ring-out ports. This is a desirable feature for UTP systems because the RJ45 connectors used on UTP cable are not usually self-shorting.

Removing a cable in this way effectively *increases* the length of

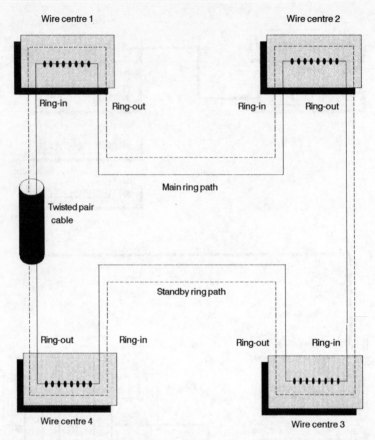

Figure 4.3 Schematic of the physical ring. Two concentric physical rings are formed when the 'last' wire centre is connected back to the 'first' wire centre.

cable in the ring and must therefore be considered in the network design. The design rules and formulae shown in Chapters 5 and 6 take into consideration the increase in cable lengths as a result of disconnecting or looping back the ring-in and ring-out ports.

Wire centres (hubs): node connections and management

Node connections

The wire centre provides the access to and connection of the node (or lobe) cables and is usually installed in standard 19 inch communications racks in the wiring closet. Near the top of the rack there are normally one or two distribution panels under which will be fitted from one to twelve wire centres of the standard 8-node type. In

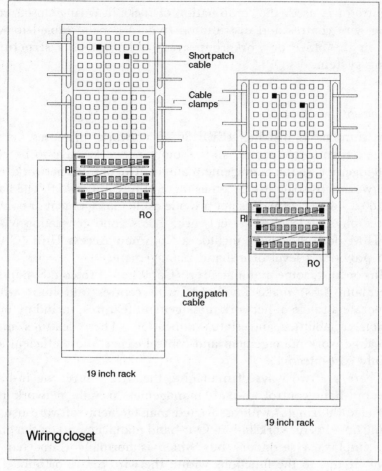

RI : Ring-in   RO : Ring-out

Figure 4.4 Wire centres and distribution (patch) panels mounted in 19 inch communication racks as part of a structured cabling system. Note that the figure shows how the cables are connected, not how they should be routed.

general, patch cables will connect the node (lobe) ports of the wire centre to a designated connector on the distribution panel, as shown in Figure 4.4. Cables will run from the back of the distribution panel to wall plates in the respective offices to connect the local PC to the ring.

There are several types of IEEE 802.5 compliant wire centres from different manufacturers. Products vary from single node (or lobe) extenders to the IBM-style 8-node unit, which is the *de-facto* standard for a single wire centre, to multinode wiring concentrators with capacities of 40, 80, 100 (or even more) nodes. Whichever type of concentrator is used, the combination of racks in wiring closets containing wire centres and distribution (patch) panels, cabled to wall plates in the office or workgroup area, is known as a **structured cabling system**.

Management

As the number of installed IEEE 802.5 networks increases, as the average network size grows, and as more networks have to be connected together, so the management and control of these networks and the network infrastructure becomes increasingly important. The basic IEEE 802.5 wire centre does not provide cable management or control over the physical level of the network. The second generation MAU from IBM does, however, include a **Common Access Unit** (CAU) which provides a level of in-band management.

In contrast, some manufacturers (Cabletron, Proteon, Synoptics, Ungermann-Bass) make intelligent wire centres and hubs which incorporate a range of network management features, including node isolation capabilities and status indication. These features make physical network management and control easier, more efficient and certainly cost-effective.

There are two ways of managing the wire centre: via in-band and/or out-band control. In-band management uses the network itself to manage the ring(s) with associated management software usually running on a PC or workstation. Out-band management, on the other hand, employs a secondary bus which is normally connected via control circuits to the functions within the wire centre or hub. This enables the network manager to isolate nodes, wire centres or even whole sections of the ring, even if the network is not responding to in-band commands. Although a high level of control is possible with only one type of control, equipment that has both in-band and out-band management capabilities will offer the highest network availability.

Switches and status LEDs are sometimes provided directly on the wire centre or concentrator modules, depending on the manufacturer. Typical features include:

- Lobe ports   LED indication of node status (in or out of ring)
                        manual in ring/out ring switch

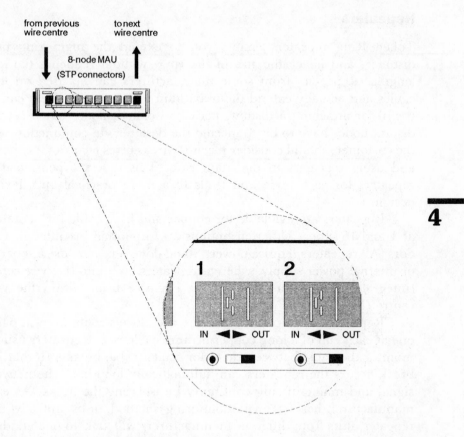

Figure 4.5   MAU node ports showing how lights and switches improve control and show the status at a glance.

- Ring-in   LED indication of normal/loopback mode

                        manual switch for normal/loopback select

- Ring-out   LED indication of normal/loopback mode

                        manual switch for normal/loopback select

- Additional LEDs   power on/off

                        system OK

as shown in Figure 4.5.

Repeaters

Token Ring repeaters enable you to extend the main ring path distance, and hence the size of the ring, without reducing the lobe lengths. Repeaters from some manufacturers can be used on lobe cables and actually extend the maximum lobe lengths. These can be useful for attaching a distant, perhaps isolated, node, but if several distant nodes have to be connected the designer, in conjunction with the customer, should consider placing wire centres near to these nodes and using repeaters in the main ring. This is less expensive than repeaters for each node and leads to a more practical and flexible design.

Repeaters are available for copper and fibre cable for operation at 4 and 16 Mbps. Different options are supported by different vendors. All repeaters require power. Standalone repeaters use a separate or internal power supply, whereas repeaters built into the wire centre (integral repeaters) use the power available from within the wire centre (MAU).

Repeaters used in the main ring are always configured in pairs: one at each end of a long copper or fibre cable run. Repeaters usually monitor the cable between them for faults (cable breaks) so that if a break occurs the repeaters can automatically loop back the network signal and maintain ring continuity by isolating the break. As each manufacturer has its own monitoring method, it is unlikely that repeater units from different manufacturers will 'talk' to one another. Hence repeaters from the same manufacturer should be used at each end of the cable. However, repeaters from different manufacturers can be mixed on the same ring, albeit over separate cable runs.

Wire centres that support integral repeaters result in simpler designs and use less cabling than designs based on external repeaters. Integral repeaters do not require a separate power supply and can be managed as part of the associated wire centre. Wiring concentrators, or hubs, invariably support integral repeaters because the hub has all the components necessary to connect the repeaters directly to the ring (i.e. power, backplane access and network connection).

Some manufacturers have incorporated many more features into their products than is necessary for IEEE 802.5 compliance, offering integral repeaters, comprehensive management systems, in-band and out-band control and mixed media support. This means that users can choose the best solution for their particular application in nearly all cases.

The distances that can be supported by adding repeaters vary depending on the manufacturer, type of cable and network speed (data rate). Repeater to repeater distances should always be taken from manufacturer's data supplied with the equipment or as separate planning information.

4.3   Customer and site requirements

4

Physical topology

Token Ring LANs can be designed in many different physical configurations which would all provide the functions specified by the customer. Although these vary, they can be classified according to whether they produce centralized or distributed wiring systems.

The **single, centralized wiring closet** cabling system simplifies design and can be easier to manage, but may use cabling less efficiently than a multi-closet design.

Note that several vendors supply workgroup wire centres or **lobe extenders** which can reduce cabling costs and improve flexibility, particularly in centralized wiring closet systems, because they enable you to expand the network without redesign and provide expansion of up to two, four or eight nodes from one lobe cable.

Distributed wiring closet cabling systems place wire centres closer to user groups. These require less cable, generally, than centralized closet designs and can be expanded quite easily. However, the maximum lobe length from the wire centre to the furthest node will be reduced in proportion to the distance between wiring closets. This may not be a limitation as the wire centres are now closer to the users. (Repeaters can also be used between wiring closets to extend the MLL for larger networks.)

Free-standing wire centres can be installed where the number of users does not justify the costs of wiring closets and racks or where these cannot be accommodated. For planning purposes, free-standing wire centres should be treated as being in separate wiring closets.

All robust working topologies, from fully distributed to fully centralized, are valid. The final choice should be based on meeting the customer, site, cost and future growth requirements, as discussed earlier. There are no 'wrong' designs if these criteria are met.

Networks should be designed to give the required level of functionality and flexibility at a reasonable cost.

Site and office layouts

Office layouts, site plans, building schematics and all relevant drawings should be evaluated with the customer to determine where wiring closets are to be placed. Any restrictions on either the number of closets or the ability to site them in certain locations should be noted. Any existing cable conduits should be checked to ensure that new or existing wiring closets can access them and they are not full.

Fibre optic cable should be considered for all external runs to protect against environmental disturbance (e.g. lightning) and to eliminate earth potential difference problems.

Token Ring designs based on a mixed fibre and UTP cable plan are particularly suitable for today's multi-storey offices and buildings. A vertical riser cable (fibre optic) can be connected to wire centres in a wiring closet on each floor. These can be linked to nodes, workgroup wire centres or lobe extenders sited at the respective office locations, using UTP for the horizontal cabling. This type of layout can considerably reduce the amount of cabling required per floor and simplifies network design.

Present and future site details should be fully investigated and a full site survey undertaken before any network designs are finalized.

4.4   Locating wiring closets

We can now consider placing the wiring closets. They should be located to give the best balance between backbone cable lengths and expected lobe lengths. A central wiring closet design will give rise to longer lobe lengths but can be expensive in cabling terms and difficult to expand unless workgroup wire centres or lobe extenders are planned. Distributed wiring closet designs may reduce the lobe lengths but as the wiring closet is closer to the nodes this means that node cables will almost certainly be within the MLL. In addition, such designs are often more cost-effective and easier to expand.

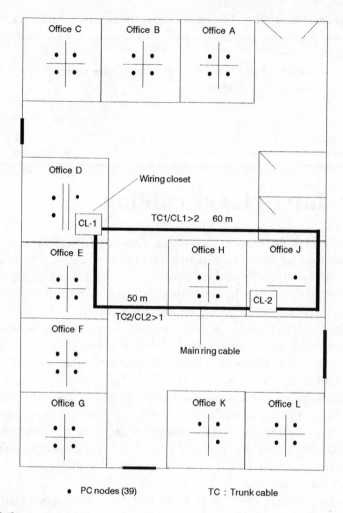

Figure 4.6 Sample office layout showing the main ring cable which forms the backbone of the ring.

The positions of wiring closets will depend on the availability of rooms in existing buildings and the proposed layouts for new buildings. Existing wiring closets or communication rooms may be full and unable to support additional racks. In this case the alternatives would be to enlarge the room or choose a different location for the wiring closet.

Having considered the factors and discussed the requirements with the customer, we should now be able to position the wiring closet or closets.

With these points in mind, mark the proposed position(s) of all wiring closets on the site layouts. Note that these positions could change when the final planning is done and maximum cable distances are calculated.

Our sample office network uses two wiring closets which are positioned as shown in Figure 4.6.

4.5   Inter-closet cabling

After you have positioned the wiring closets you will need to connect them together to form the network backbone. Cable for linking wiring closets will be IBM Type 1 or equivalent on STP networks, Level 3, 4 or 5 on UTP networks (see Appendix A), fibre optic or any combination of these, depending on the application.

The length of cable between wiring closets has to be allowed for when verifying the network to see if it will work. This is included, or taken into consideration, in the design formulae we will be using in the following chapters. We therefore need to know these lengths fairly accurately, which means we must know how the cables are routed. If a site survey is not possible, or has not been carried out yet, or if we are in the initial phases of the design, then we can use the distance scale on the layouts to determine the length of the inter-closet runs. Do not forget the vertical rises and drops.

We can now add the cables to the cable schedule.

In some areas cable may have to be fire-resistant or fire-proof, depending on the local safety regulations. Check to ensure that the appropriate cable has been provisioned as this will affect the capital equipment costs.

For the purpose of this example we have assumed that the inter-closet cable in our sample office network is run in conduits, as shown in Figure 4.6.

Now we can also complete the wiring closet schedule shown in Figure 4.7.

The actual planning and positioning of the wiring closets does not take much time. The time is taken up in completing the forms (usually the case!). However, this is necessary if we are to manage the network and associated designs professionally. We can – and often do – verify that the design is 'good' before completing all the forms. In the following chapters we show you how to verify your design; you can use the formulae to check lobe lengths whenever necessary.

Wiring closet schedule

Designer [   ]   Date [   ]

Network no. [   ]   Page no. [   ] of [   ]

| Wiring closet | Location | Qty racks | Interconnection | |
			From	To
CL-1	Inside office D	1	CL-2	CL-2
CL-2	Inside office J	1	CL-1	CL-1

4

Figure 4.7 Wiring closet schedule for the sample office layout.

In the next section we look at selecting wire centres, routing node cables and completing the associated schedules. The schedule forms may be completed at a later stage in the design, if you wish. The order in which these design stages are undertaken can vary according to each designer's preference. If you intend to complete the forms later you should ensure you have enough information to continue with the verification and to complete the schedules when required.

4.6 Locating wire centres (MAUs) and racks

Now that we have located the wiring closets it is possible to determine the number and placement of wire centres and hence racks. For eight-node wire centres, divide the number of nodes by eight and round up to the nearest whole number. This will give you the minimum number of wire centres required. A similar calculation can be done for multiport hubs to determine the number of node port modules, or even complete hubs, that will be needed on larger rings.

Allocating wire centres to wiring closets

If you have not already done so, at this stage you can draw in all cables from the nodes to their associated wiring closets (lobe cables) on the site layouts.

When we verify the design we will need to know the lengths of cable runs from node to wire centre (or hub) port. It is important, therefore, to ensure that these lengths are accurate on the drawings. For the sample office layout we have shown the node cables run in conduits (Figure 4.8), from which we can determine the lobe lengths. These are itemized in the cable schedule shown in Figure 4.9.

To determine the number of wire centres per closet, we have used the number of nodes connected to each closet, divided this by eight and rounded up to the next whole number. We can now add together the number of wire centres in every wiring closet to give the total number of wire centres required for the sample office network design.

It is possible to increase this number to allow for growth and to build in a certain amount of redundancy. However, as we will see

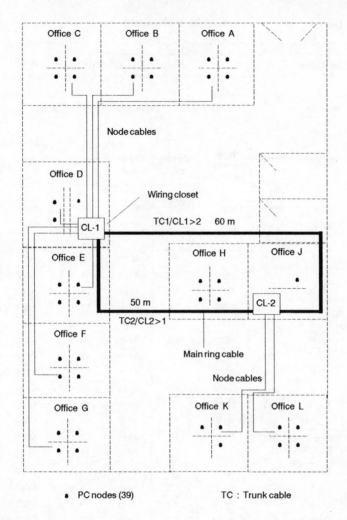

Figure 4.8 Node (lobe) cable runs in the sample office layout. The node cables can be run in conduits.

shortly from the design rules, the maximum number of 8-node wire centres in a single ring should not exceed 33, to accommodate a maximum of 260 nodes. Whilst 260-node rings can be designed, it is recognized that for ease of management and control, ring sizes should be limited to 100 nodes per ring or less.

Determining the number of racks

There is space for up to twelve 8-node (host) wire centres in a single 19 inch rack allowing for patch panels (at the top) and power supplies

(a)   Cable schedule

Designer [   ]   Date [   ]

Network no. [1]   Page no. [1] of [2]

Name	Phone no.	Node address Low 2 bytes	Cable no.	Cable length	From	To
Trunk 1	N/A	N/A	TC1	60 m	CL-1	CL-2
Trunk 2	N/A	N/A	TC2	50 m	CL-2	CL-1
Acc1	241	F34C	A1	45 m	CL-1	Adp1
Acc2	233	AA33	A2	45 m	CL-1	Adp2
Acc3	265	3D4F	A3	45 m	CL-1	Adp3
Acc4	211	267B	A4	45 m	CL-1	Adp4
Acc5	276	3FF5	B1	35 m	CL-1	Bdp1
Acc6	266	4C33	B2	35 m	CL-1	Bdp2
Acc7	289	A345	B3	35 m	CL-1	Bdp3
Acc8	219	B654	B4	35 m	CL-1	Bdp4
Acc9	269	CC45	C1	35 m	CL-1	Cdp1
Acc10	292	A3BC	C2	35 m	CL-1	Cdp2
Acc11	255	4FCC	C3	35 m	CL-1	Cdp3
Acc12	213	E4A3	C4	35 m	CL-1	Cdp4
Per1	222	A342	D1	10 m	CL-1	Ddp1
Per2	262	B555	D2	10 m	CL-1	Ddp2
Per3	273	5FF3	E1	10 m	CL-1	Edp1
Per4	237	AFF4	E2	10 m	CL-1	Edp2
Per5	271	BDFA	E3	10 m	CL-1	Edp3
Per6	252	ACDD	E4	10 m	CL-1	Edp4
Per7	284	A1DF	F1	40 m	CL-1	Fdp1
Per8	299	F3FF	F2	40 m	CL-1	Fdp2
Per9	288	C45F	F3	40 m	CL-1	Fdp3

Figure 4.9 Cable schedule for the sample office layout: (a) Page 1, and (b) Page 2. It is important to use a standard numbering scheme or one agreed by everyone.

(at the bottom). The number of racks per wiring closet can be calculated by dividing the number of rack mounted wire centres in each closet by 12 and rounding the result up to the next whole number.

(b)   **Cable schedule**

Designer [   ]   Date [   ]

Network no. [1]   Page no. [2] of [2]

4

Name	Phone no.	Node address Low 2 bytes	Cable no.	Cable length	From	To
Per10	251	7FB4	F4	35 m	CL-1	Fdp4
Per11	223	B41F	G1	60 m	CL-1	Gdp1
Per12	244	665A	G2	60 m	CL-1	Gdp2
Per13	281	3AD5	G3	60 m	CL-1	Gdp3
Per14	283	33DF	G4	60 m	CL-1	Gdp4
MIS1	277	F67A	H1	15 m	CL-2	Hdp1
MIS2	231	34AA	H2	15 m	CL-2	Hdp2
MIS3	245	2FFF	H3	15 m	CL-2	Hdp3
MIS4	256	67AC	H4	15 m	CL-2	Hdp4
Serv1	267	1ABC	J1	15 m	CL-2	Jdp1
Sale1	212	2DEF	K1	20 m	CL-2	Kdp1
Sale2	223	D3FF	K2	20 m	CL-2	Kdp2
Sale3	291	4DA5	K3	20 m	CL-2	Kdp3
Sale4	287	6CCC	K4	20 m	CL-2	Kdp4
Sale5	247	FC4A	L1	20 m	CL-2	Ldp1
Sale6	259	AD34	L2	20 m	CL-2	Ldp2
Sale7	272	AD99	L3	20 m	CL-2	Ldp3
Sale8	216	AC59	L4	20 m	CL-2	Ldp4

Figure 4.9 *Cont.*

Use the manufacturer's sizes for designs incorporating wiring concentrators and hubs and divide the available rack space (height) by the height of the concentrator, then round down to the nearest whole number. This will be the number of concentrators that can be mounted in a single rack.

(a)   **Rack layouts**

Designer [   ]   Date [   ]

Network no. [1   ]   Page no. [1] of [2]

Wiring closet [CL-1]   Racks [1] of [1]

Rack no.	Rk 1
MAU1	S00/C1/R1/M1
MAU2	S00/C1/R1/M2
MAU3	S00/C1/R1/M3
MAU4	S00/C1/R1/M4
MAU5	S00/C1/R1/M5
MAU6	
MAU7	
MAU8	
MAU9	
MAU10	
MAU11	
MAU12	

Rack no.	
MAU1	
MAU2	
MAU3	
MAU4	
MAU5	
MAU6	
MAU7	
MAU8	
MAU9	
MAU10	
MAU11	
MAU12	

Figure 4.10   Rack layouts for the sample office: (a) Wiring closet 1 which consists of five 8-node wire centres mounted in rack 1, and (b) Wiring closet 2 which consists of three 8-node wire centres mounted in rack 1.

The rack layouts can now be completed together with the sequence charts. Blank forms are included in Appendix C for designers to copy and use; they are based on standard 8-node wire centre units. Note that it is often useful to draw a freehand schematic of the whole network which can be used to help complete the associated forms and as a check on the network design.

For the sample office, we have included examples of the rack layouts showing five wire centres in wiring closet 1 and three wire

(b) **Rack layouts**

Designer [   ]   Date [   ]

Network no. [1]   Page no. [2] of [2]

Wiring closet [CL-2]   Racks [1] of [1]

4

Rack no.	Rk 1
MAU1	S00/C2/R1/M1
MAU2	S00/C2/R1/M2
MAU3	S00/C2/R1/M3
MAU4	
MAU5	
MAU6	
MAU7	
MAU8	
MAU9	
MAU10	
MAU11	
MAU12	

Rack no.	
MAU1	
MAU2	
MAU3	
MAU4	
MAU5	
MAU6	
MAU7	
MAU8	
MAU9	
MAU10	
MAU11	
MAU12	

Figure 4.10 *Cont.*

centres in wiring closet 2. See Figures 4.10a and b. The numbering systems used in our examples are for illustration only. You can use any numbering scheme as long as it clearly identifies all components and is fully documented.

Wire centre interconnection

The interconnection of wire centres and hubs should reflect the physical ring topology seen in earlier chapters as shown in the wire centre sequence charts. See Figures 4.11a and b. The additional

(a) Wire centre sequence chart

Designer [   ] Date [   ]

Network no. [1] Page no. [1] of [1]

Wiring closet [CL-1] Rack no. [1]

	Ring-in			Ring-out	
From MAU	C2/R1/M3	Wire centre no.	C1/R1/M1	C1/R1/M2	To MAU
Length	60 m	Longest lobe cable	45 m	Patch	Length
From MAU	C1/R1/M1	Wire centre no.	C1/R1/M2	C1/R1/M3	To MAU
Length	Patch	Longest lobe cable	35 m	Patch	Length
From MAU	C1/R1/M2	Wire centre no.	C1/R1/M3	C1/R1/M4	To MAU
Length	Patch	Longest lobe cable	10 m	Patch	Length
From MAU	C1/R1/M3	Wire centre no.	C1/R1/M4	C1/R1/M5	To MAU
Length	Patch	Longest lobe cable	40 m	Patch	Length
From MAU	C1/R1/M4	Wire centre no.	C1/R1/M5	C2/R1/M1	To MAU
Length	Patch	Longest lobe cable	60 m	50 m	Length
From MAU		Wire centre no.			To MAU
Length		Longest lobe cable			Length
From MAU		Wire centre no.			To MAU
Length		Longest lobe cable			Length
From MAU		Wire centre no.			To MAU
Length		Longest lobe cable			Length
From MAU		Wire centre no.			To MAU
Length		Longest lobe cable			Length
From MAU		Wire centre no.			To MAU
Length		Longest lobe cable			Length
From MAU		Wire centre no.			To MAU
Length		Longest lobe cable			Length
From MAU		Wire centre no.			To MAU
Length		Longest lobe cable			Length

Figure 4.11 MAU interconnection for the sample office: (a) Wire closet 1, and (b) Wire closet 2. Node (lobe) lengths will be compared with the distance found from our maximum lobe length calculations.

components can now be included on the equipment schedule. The quantities of racks, wire centres etc., required for the sample office are shown in the equipment schedule. See Figure 4.12.

(b) **Wire centre sequence chart**

Designer		Date	

Network no.	1	Page no.	1	of	1

Wiring closet	CL-2	Rack no.	1

	Ring-in					Ring-out	
From MAU	C1/R1/M5	Wire centre no.		C2/R1/M1	C2/R1/M2	To MAU
Length	50 m	Longest lobe cable		45 m	Patch	Length
From MAU	C2/R1/M1	Wire centre no.		C2/R1/M2	C2/R1/M3	To MAU
Length	Patch	Longest lobe cable		35 m	Patch	Length
From MAU	C2/R1/M2	Wire centre no.		C2/R1/M3	C1/R1/M1	To MAU
Length	Patch	Longest lobe cable		10 m	60 m	Length
From MAU		Wire centre no.				To MAU
Length		Longest lobe cable				Length
From MAU		Wire centre no.				To MAU
Length		Longest lobe cable				Length
From MAU		Wire centre no.				To MAU
Length		Longest lobe cable				Length
From MAU		Wire centre no.				To MAU
Length		Longest lobe cable				Length
From MAU		Wire centre no.				To MAU
Length		Longest lobe cable				Length
From MAU		Wire centre no.				To MAU
Length		Longest lobe cable				Length
From MAU		Wire centre no.				To MAU
Length		Longest lobe cable				Length
From MAU		Wire centre no.				To MAU
Length		Longest lobe cable				Length
From MAU		Wire centre no.				To MAU
Length		Longest lobe cable				Length

Figure 4.11 *Cont.*

4.7 Verifying the design

Having completed the forms at this stage, or decided to do this later, we need to determine whether the design is a good working one. If

Equipment schedule

Designer		Date	

Network no.	1	Page no.	1	of	1

Item	Part no.	Quantity	Price
PC-bus I/F			
PC/AT-bus I/F		39	
MCA I/F			
EISA-bus I/F			
Boot ROMs			
Wire centres		8	
Power supply		2	
Power supply			
19" racks		2	
Data cable STP	Type 1	110 m	
Data cable UTP			
Patch cables (3 m)		6	
Patch cables (10 m)			
Adapter cables		39	
Fibre optic cable			
Other items 1			
Other items 2			
		Total	

Figure 4.12 Equipment schedule showing additional items.

it is, then a single node, attached anywhere on the network, will be able to transmit data reliably round the whole ring. This is the design criterion we are working to and, to see if our design meets it, we need to know the maximum distance any node can be from its associated wire centre or hub. We can then compare this with the actual node distances (lobe lengths) in the network. If they are *less* than the calculated figure, the design will work.

The MLL is easily determined from tables or formulae corresponding to your network design. It is the key parameter in the design. If the MLL is within limits, the network will run – as we shall see in the next chapter. If it is not, then the design must be modified until it is.

Ways of modifying the design to increase the MLL or reduce the actual node distances in your network include:

4

(1) reducing the number of host wire centres per ring,

(2) using workgroup wire centres to reduce the effective main ring path length or lobe extenders if only one or two nodes are affected,

(3) adding copper or fibre repeaters,.

(4) repositioning wiring closets.

The most practical and cost-effective method should be chosen.

We can now look at the derivation and application of the design rules and formulae for verifying our network design(s). This will enable us to calculate the MLL for any design and, by comparing this with the actual node distances, determine whether the network will work.

Token Ring networks can be designed using any combination of UTP, STP and fibre cabling within a single ring as a result of the point-to-point nature of ring topologies. For ease of design, maintenance and growth, it is recommended that rings using mixed media types should separate the different media segments with UTP, STP or fibre repeaters. The MLL for each segment can then be calculated, independently of all other segments, using the appropriate formula for that segment.

In Chapter 5 we look at the design rules and formulae for STP-based networks or parts of networks (segments). In Chapter 6 we look at the design rules and formulae for UTP-based networks or parts of networks (segments). In Chapter 7 we look at the design rules and formulae for fibre-based networks or parts of networks (segments).

5

Verifying the design: rules and formulae for STP cabling

CHAPTER CONTENTS

Chapter summary

In this chapter we introduce the formula method for calculating the MLL of a Token Ring network consisting of STP cable for the whole ring or for an STP ring segment. The advantages and disadvantages of the central versus distributed wiring closet design are discussed and the basic design rules are explained.

The design rules, when followed, remove several factors from the planning considerations and hence make it easier for the network planner to design the ring. This is possible because within a structured cabling system certain elements can be allowed for (e.g. patch cable and adapter cable losses), leaving the designer to concentrate on the placement of closets, repeaters and nodes in the knowledge that the formulae will include the other parameters.

The chapter also introduces the three ring topologies – single closet, multiple closet and multiple closet with repeaters – and shows you how to calculate the maximum lobe length in each case. Several worked examples are included for each topology at both 4 and 16 Mbps bit rates.

We also look at how a centralized, single closet design can greatly simplify the planning process by using the MLL corresponding to a maximum size ring for all such designs. This is a very popular design because no further calculations are needed provided that the furthest node is within the set MLL.

The chapter then goes on to discuss multiple wiring closet topologies explaining the terms **adjusted ring length** for multiple closet designs without repeaters and **drive distance** for ring designs with repeaters. As each new concept and topology is introduced, the planning rules are extended to allow for known variables so that the design process stays as straightforward as possible. Detailed illustrated examples are included in each case showing how the MLL is calculated for networks running at 4 and 16 Mbps.

5

We then consider rings with workgroup wire centres and show how these can further simplify network design and save on network cabling. New designs and extensions to existing networks can be accommodated with the workgroup wire centre, making it a very attractive choice for applications that might experience a high rate of additions, moves and changes.

The chapter concludes by taking the sample office network and calculating the MLL to determine whether the planned network is a working configuration.

5.1   Introduction

In this chapter we show you how to verify the design (Step 5 in the design stages) for your network, or segments of your network, utilizing shielded twisted pair (STP) cabling. First we compare the two main methods for verifying designs: distance tables versus formulae. Both methods allow us to find the MLL for a given configuration – the criterion which will decide whether our design will produce a working network or not!

Next we introduce the general formula for verifying Token Ring designs. From this, by applying common-sense rules applicable to structured cabling systems (which we will itemize), we produce a simple formula for each type of network topology as discussed in earlier chapters and briefly reiterated below.

We then show how the appropriate formula is used to calculate the MLL for each of the major topologies you are likely to encounter, using illustrated examples at both 4 and 16 Mbps:

- single wiring closet topology   (Section 5.2)
- multiple wiring closet topology without repeaters   (Section 5.3)
- multiple wiring closet topology with repeaters   (Section 5.4)
- network design using workgroup wire centres   (Section 5.5).

Finally we use the formula to calculate the MLL for our sample office layout to verify that our design works!

5.1.1 Design formulae versus distance tables

Token Ring products that are fully compatible with the IBM Token Ring network may be designed by following the recommendations and using the tables in the IBM Token Ring network Introduction and Planning Guide (Part No. GA27-3677-2).

Token Ring networks can also be designed using the rules and formulae described in this and the following chapters. The formulae method has the following advantages:

- easier to use and understand
- direct indication of maximum lobe length
- rules and formulae are more consistent for varying topologies, data rates and media
- easily adapted for different types of MAU and NIC.

The following points should be noted when designing Token Ring networks with the formulae, some of which give rise to differences in maximum lobe length calculations when compared with the IBM tables:

- Non-IBM MAUs may have different loss budgets to IBM MAUs.

- Repeaters are available integrated within the MAU or as standalone, rack mounted units. Designs based on standalone repeaters must take into consideration the cable between the repeater and associated MAU.

- Tables are usually produced for a specific set of equipment whereas the formulae can be selected for many types of equipment.

If networks are designed using the IBM tables, *be careful*; table entries for networks with repeaters refer to a different distance than the table entries for networks without repeaters.

The design formulae in this guide always calculate the maximum lobe length.

5

5.1.2   Network topologies

We saw that the flexibility inherent in the Token Ring architecture in relation to network topologies and layouts gives rise to several ways of designing networks. One design is to have a central wiring closet and to connect all nodes in a physical star configuration (though still a logical ring) as shown in Figure 5.1a. An alternative design is to have two or more wiring closets situated as close as possible to concentrations of users that need to be connected to the ring, as shown in Figure 5.1b.

Small rings are relatively easy to design and often only need a single closet. In contrast, large rings may require two or more wiring closets connected directly by cable, by cable and repeaters, or by fibre.

We will look at each of these configurations and, together with the design recommendations, show how the formula is applied to calculate the MLL in each case.

5.1.3   General formula

The derivation of the general formula is included in Appendix B. This formula allows us to calculate the MLL for our network or segment from a knowledge of the maximum cable budget and the respective component losses:

(a) Single wiring closet network design

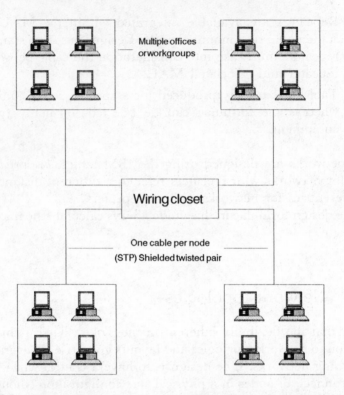

Figure 5.1 Network design based on: (a) Single wiring closet in which all nodes are connected to a central point, and (b) Multiple wiring closets in which the wiring closets can be located close to workgroups to minimize cable costs. Note that in (b) the main ring cable length is included in the MLL calculations.

$$MLL = MCB - K1 * M - K2 * C - MRL$$

where:

MLL	:	maximum lobe length
MCB	:	maximum cable budget
K1, K2	:	constants
M	:	number of MAUs
C	:	number of wiring closets
MRL	:	main ring path length.

The maximum cable budget is a function of the signal drive capability of the adapter card and is provided by the manufacturer.

(b) Multiple wiring closet network design

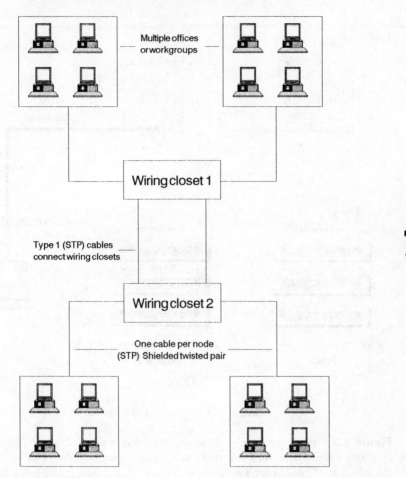

5

Figure 5.1   *Cont.*

For further details see Appendix B. The main ring path length is the sum of all lengths of cable that make up the main ring (i.e. *not* including node cables).

The general formula can be simplified for STP Token Ring networks and segments by applying the following recommendations in your design. This will ensure that predictable losses, which can affect the cable budget and MLL in structured cabling systems, can be taken into consideration wherever possible. The network designer then only has to consider the site-dependent drop cable lengths, the MLL from the formula, as shown in Figure 5.2.

Note that some of the parameters referred to in the recommendations can be reduced (e.g. patch cable lengths) to increase the

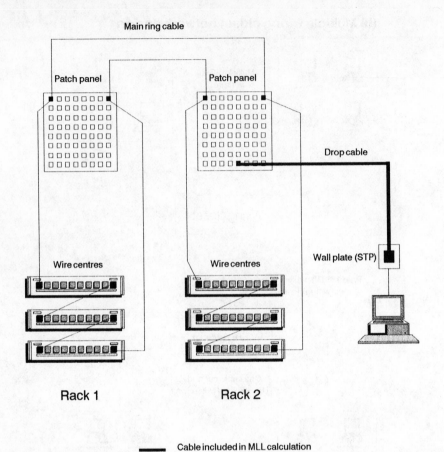

Figure 5.2   Single wiring closet without repeaters – use Formula A. Example of a 16 Mbps ring design with two racks in a single closet. At a data rate of 16 Mbps, the MCB is 180 m. From Formula A:

$$MLL = 180 - 9 * M - 10 * L$$
$$= 180 - 54 - 20 = 106 \text{ m}$$

maximum lobe length. Take care to ensure that any changes to the recommendations are valid (e.g. from manufacturer's data) and that they reflect the actual installation, otherwise it could result in incorrect network designs. Some parameters cannot be changed as these are fixed by physical or electrical limitations.

Table 5.1 summarizes the Token Ring planning rules for STP single ring designs. By adopting the recommendations, the network installation will conform to recognized high standards.

Table 5.1 Token Ring planning rules for single ring, STP designs.

Rule 1	Maximum number of nodes supported is 260
Rule 2	Maximum number of 8-node MAUs is 33
Rule 3	Maximum number of 8-node MAUs per rack is 12
Rule 4	Within a rack, connect MAUs to each other with 3 metres, or shorter, Type 6 patch cables
Rule 5	Connect MAU lobe ports to the distribution panel within a rack with 3 metres, or shorter, Type 6 patch cables
Rule 6	Connect MAUs in different racks within the same wiring closet with 10 metres, or shorter, Type 6 patch cables
Rule 7	Connections from the back of the distribution panel to the wall plate in the work area should be made with Type 1 (or Type 2) cable
Rule 8	Connections from the wall plate in the work area to the node adapter can use 3 metres, or shorter, Type 6 patch cables

5

The general formula then becomes:

$$MLL = MCB - 9M - 5C - MRL$$

where:

K1 : 9 (assumes 3 m patching cable plus 8-node MAU insertion loss equivalent to 6 m Type 1 cable)

K2 : 5 (length of cable equivalent to the connector losses between two or more wiring closets).

5.2 Single wiring closet networks without repeaters

With a single wiring closet network it is possible to define a special case configuration where the distance to the furthest node is set to a maximum allowable cable length. This gives a design that 'always works' for networks operating at 4 and 16 Mbps. As the maximum node or lobe length is set, we will not need the formula or distance tables for this special configuration.

We call this the single closet, no formula network design. It is possible because the worst case distance is typically 85 to 100 m (lobe length), which is sufficient for most installations. If the exact MLL must be known or longer lobe lengths are required, then we can still use the respective formulae to calculate it. This approach greatly simplifies network design enabling you to plan Token Ring systems without a detailed knowledge of the technology.

The 'no-formula' method can be extended to multiple closet networks with repeaters, if repeaters are used between all closets, enabling designers to plan large and more complex rings just as quickly and easily as single closet networks. (When all wiring closets are interconnected via repeater links, each closet can be treated as a single closet network (segment) for planning purposes. If repeaters are integrated into wire centres this will simplify the topology and hence the network planning requirements.)

If the MLL for single wiring closet networks has to be calculated, then we can use a formula (or tables) to determine the maximum lobe length for a given configuration. We call this the single wiring closet design, with formula. We look at each of these in turn, with examples.

5.2.1   Single wiring closet, no formula network design

If all lobe cables terminate in a single wiring closet and the above rules are adopted, then the ring will have a positive cable budget provided that the drop cable to any node does not exceed 100 m for operation at 4 Mbps or 80 m (for single rings with up to 100 nodes) at 16 Mbps. (The drop cable is the cable that connects the distribution panel in the wiring closet to the wall plate in the work area.)

These values are based on maximum cable budgets of 390 m and 180 m, for 4 and 16 Mbps operation, respectively, as being representative of distances achievable by most manufacturers. The manufacturer's published MCBs should be used in the formulae if exact values for the MLL are required or if long lobe lengths are envisaged.

If wiring concentrators are planned, then their capacities, and hence sizes, will depend on the manufacturer. Use the manufacturer's data to determine the number and placement of concentrators and hence the number of racks required.

Single closet network designs make up a large percentage of all network configurations. Whilst it is necessary for advanced design engineers and consultants to be able to plan networks based on more complex topologies, and details are included in this guide to enable them to do this, many network applications can be satisfied using the single wiring closet designs, which are very simple to plan.

5.2.2 Single wiring closet design using the formula

There will be applications where the distance to the farthest node has to be calculated beforehand to determine the network feasibility. In these cases we can use Formula A to calculate the MLL for a given configuration. Note that for all Token Ring networks the design should avoid placing nodes at distances approaching the MLL as this will limit the future expansion capabilities of your network. It is better to site wire centres closer to the work areas, thus having two or more wiring closets, and to keep drop lengths shorter if you expect your network to grow.

5

With our STP network (or segment) designed to conform with Rules 1 to 8, we can then calculate the MLL for a single closet network design using Formula A:

Formula A: $MLL = MCB - 9*M - 10*L$

where:

MCB : maximum cable budget
M   : number of wire centres (MAUs)
L   : number of long patch cables.

In the formula, all distances are given in metres.

In Formula A our main ring path length is the length of all long cables linking wire centres between racks, as shown in the example of Figure 5.2. If the size of the network requires only a single rack, as is often the case when concentrators are used, then Formula A reduces to:

$MLL = MCB - 9*M$

Examples of typical, single rack configurations are shown in Figures 5.3 and 5.4.

Use the value for MCB equivalent to the data rate and wire centre type you will be running on your network. Typical values are shown in Table 5.2.

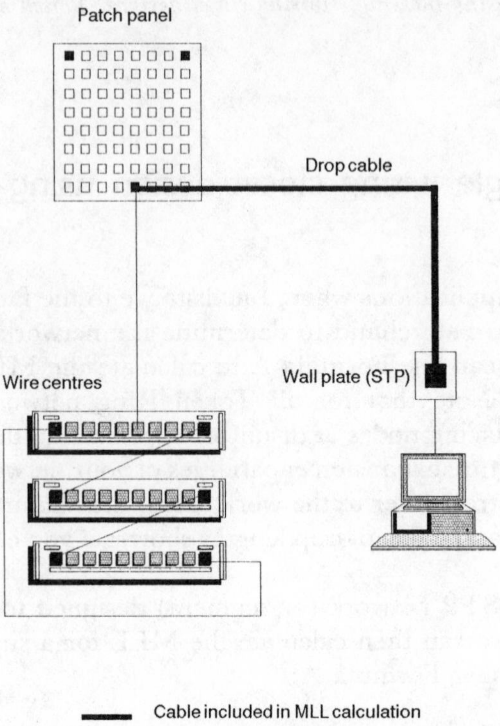

Figure 5.3 Single wiring closet without repeaters – use Formula A. Example of a 4 Mbps ring design. At 4 Mbps the MCB is 390 m. From Formula A:

$$\begin{aligned} MLL &= 390 - 9 * M - 10 * L \\ &= 390 - 27 - 0 = 363 \text{ m} \end{aligned}$$

If the MLL from the above calculation is less than the longest node in your network it may be possible to redesign the network to use multiple wiring closets (with or without repeaters), or workgroup wire centres to place wire centres closer to the work areas. Single wiring closet networks are easier to design and maintain than multiple wiring closet networks, making them the preferred choice for some network planners. However, there will be applications where multiple closets are necessary and in these cases we may or may not decide

Table 5.2 Maximum cable budgets for STP (IBM Type 1) designs.

Data rate	MCB
4 Mbps	390 m
16 Mbps	180 m

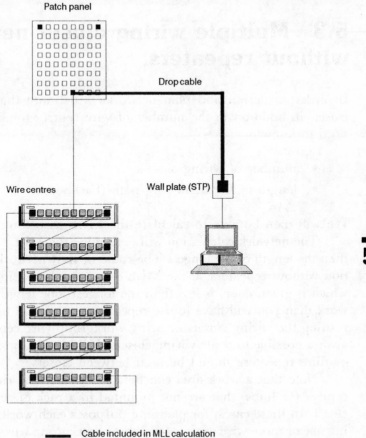

5

Figure 5.4   Single wiring closet without repeaters – use Formula A. Example of a 16 Mbps ring design using a single wiring closet. At this data rate, the MCB is 180 m. From Formula A:

$$MLL = 180 - 9 * M - 10 * L$$
$$= 180 - 54 - 0 = 126 \, m$$

to use repeaters, depending on the lobe distances required and the application. Hence we can now consider networks using two or more wiring closets connected either directly or via copper repeaters. Designs based on fibre repeaters are discussed in Chapter 7 but the principles are identical to those for copper repeater designs.

5.3 Multiple wiring closet networks without repeaters

In order to design and plan networks with more than one wiring closet, in addition to the number of wire centres (or hubs), we will need to know:

- number of wiring closets
- length of the main ring path (backbone).

We will then be able to calculate the MLL as before.

The network calculation will determine the MLL. If it is greater than the length of the longest lobe cable in your network, it will function without repeaters. If the MLL determined by using Formula B, which is given later, is less than the longest lobe length in your network then you will have to use repeaters or redesign the network by resiting the wiring closets or using workgroup wire centres. It is not always possible to resite wiring closets. If this is the case, then copper or fibre repeaters should be used between closets.

Note that a work area can be connected to the ring using wire centres (or hubs) that are not mounted in a rack or separate wiring closet. In these cases, for planning purposes each work area containing one or more wire centres (excluding workgroup wire centres which are a special case and discussed later) should be treated as if it were a separate wiring closet.

Standalone MAUs and hubs can be incorporated into the planning rules as follows:

Rule 9   MAUs installed in a work area should be connected to each other and to wall plates with 3 metres, or shorter, Type 6 patch cables.

Rule 10   All connections between wiring closets and from wiring closets to/from host MAUs in work areas shall be made with Type 1 (or Type 2) cable.

Determining the MRL in multiple wiring closet designs

In multiple wiring closet networks we have to consider the lengths of cable interconnecting wiring closets (and work areas if these contain additional non-workgroup wire centres) and the worst case situation with regard to the distance a packet must travel round the ring. The worst case, or longest distance, will occur if and when the main ring cable is disconnected at the first or last wire centre (or hub port) in any closet, to expand the ring or check for faults. This leads to the concept of an **adjusted ring length**.

An important aspect of the IEEE 802.5 STP cabling scheme is that the last wire centre ring-out port can be connected back to the first wire centre ring-in port, thus completing the physical loop. This creates two paths for the data signal between wire centres, as we saw earlier. In normal circumstances the primary path, known as the main ring path, carries live data while the secondary path, known as the standby ring path, acts as a backup as shown in Figure 5.5. This method of connection, together with the self-shorting plugs used on IEEE 802.5 STP rings, enables any cable in the main ring to be disconnected without disrupting the network. The signal is automatically looped back around the backup path. Consequently, the network can be reconfigured, or a section of the network can be isolated for maintenance, without having to bring the ring down.

Note that some manufacturers' MAUs have switches on the ring-in, ring-out and lobe ports enabling any port to be isolated without having physically to remove cables.

If, however, a section of the main ring is disconnected by removing the IEEE 802.5 plug (media interface connector), then the data will have to travel almost twice the distance round the ring compared with the distance it travelled before. This has to be taken into consideration when planning networks if we want the ring to continue working under these conditions. Hence, the adjusted ring length is defined as the length of the main ring path minus the shortest cable between wiring closets. (If the shortest cable is disconnected then the signal will have to travel the longest distance around the ring. This is the worst case for which we must plan.)

We can now replace the MRL term in our general formula by the ARL to give the formula for calculating the MLL in a multiple closet, no repeater design – Formula B:

Formula B: $MLL = MCB - 9 * M - 5 * C - ARL$

where:

MCB	:	maximum cable budget
M	:	number of wire centres
C	:	number of wiring closets
ARL	:	adjusted ring length

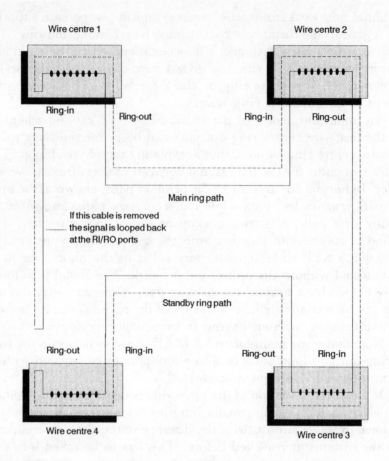

Figure 5.5 Token ring cabling topology illustrating the adjusted ring length. Removing a cable from the main ring increases the distance data has to travel. Removing the shortest cable between wiring closets will give the maximum distance that the data has to travel, that is, the ARL.

As for Formula A, all distances are in metres.

If there is more than one rack of wire centres or hubs in a closet then add ten to the ARL for every long patch cable in the network to allow for long patch cables between racks in the same closet.

Note that in multiple wiring closet designs, wherever possible the closets should be sited close to work areas, keeping lobe cables short. This gives greater flexibility, is easier to expand and assists maintenance.

Examples of multiple closet STP network designs without repeaters are shown in Figures 5.6. to 5.8.

If the MLL from the above calculation is less than the longest node in your network, it may be possible to redesign the network

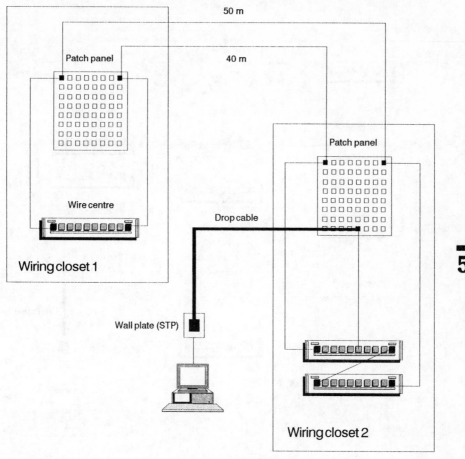

——— Cable included in MLL calculation

Figure 5.6 Multiple closets without repeaters – use Formula B. Example 4 Mbps ring design using two wiring closets. At the 4 Mbps data rate, the MCB is 390 m. From Formula B:

$$MLL = 390 - 9 * M - 5 * C - ARL$$
$$= 390 - 27 - 10 - 50 = 303 \text{ m}$$

to avoid using repeaters; some suggestions are given below. If you decide to use copper repeaters then you must use the rules and formula detailed later in Section 5.4.

- If the calculated MLL is less than the length of the longest node cable in your network it may be possible to extend the

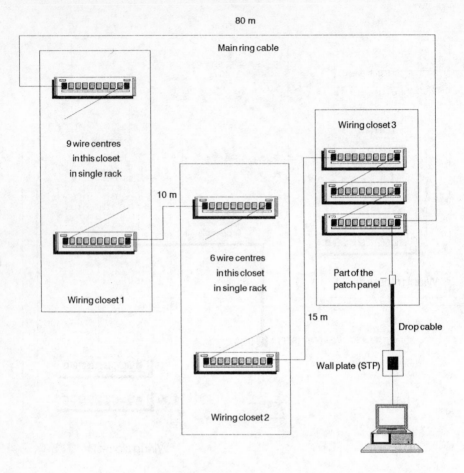

_____ Cable included in MLL calculation

Figure 5.7   Multiple closets without repeaters – use Formula B. Example 4 Mbps ring design using three wiring closets. At the 4 Mbps data rate, the MCB is 390 m. From Formula B:

$$MLL = 390 - 9 * M - 5 * C - ARL$$
$$= 390 - 162 - 15 - 95 = 118 \text{ m}$$

Note that the patch panels are not shown for clarity.

> MLL by reducing the number of wire centres in the ring, especially if additional wire centres have been included in the initial calculation to allow for growth.
>
> • You can also exchange or replace wire centres by multiport hubs, costs and application permitting. For example, a single 80-port hub can be treated as a single MAU if the ring is formed at the backplane of the hub and signals are repeated

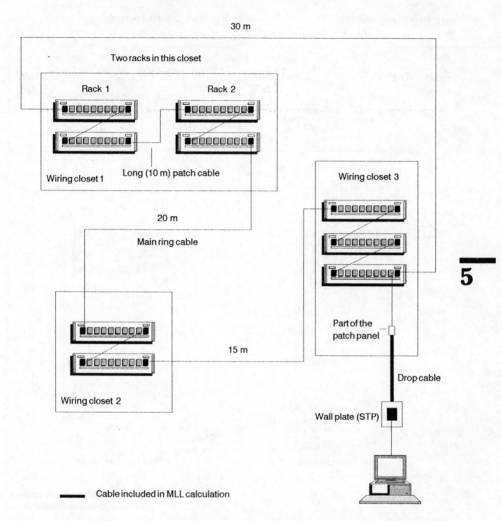

Figure 5.8 Multiple closets without repeaters – use Formula B. Example of a 16 Mbps ring design using three wiring closets. At the 16 Mbps data rate the MCB is 180 m; the ARL = 30 + 20 + 10 = 60 m. From Formula B:

$$MLL = 180 - 9*M - 5*C - ARL$$
$$= 180 - 72 - 15 - 60 = 33 \text{ m}$$

Note that the patch panels are not shown for clarity.

on the backplane. The manufacturer or supplier should be able to give details of the operation of their hub products and the associated equivalent loss.

• If the building has not been finished and the cabling has not been installed, it may be possible to change the positions of

(a) Integral repeaters   (b) Standalone repeaters

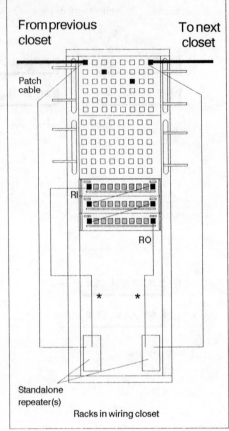

* Include the cables in ARL or drive
distance of respective formula

RI   : Ring-in
RO : Ring-out

Figure 5.9 Cabling options for Token Ring repeaters: (a) Integral repeaters can be supplied within the MAU or hub, or (b) Separate standalone units can be provided, usually mounted in the bottom of the rack. Note that the figure shows how the cables are connected, not how they should be routed.

wiring closets to place the wire centres nearer to the nodes. It may also be possible to reduce the overall number of wiring closets, which might increase the MLL.

- An alternative configuration for connecting distant nodes and for expanding networks without having to reconfigure or redesign utilizes the special features of workgroup wire centres or lobe extenders. See Section 5.5 for details on designing networks with these units.

- The ring can also be redesigned as two (or more) rings connected together by file servers, routers or bridges. Again, the cost and application requirements will have a direct bearing on this option.

Repeaters

For rings that use Type 1 or Type 2 cable in the main ring path, ring size can be increased by integrating copper repeaters into the ring-in or ring-out port(s) of their associated wire centres or hubs, depending on the manufacturer. Integral repeaters reduce the number of and lengths of cable in the main ring, thereby enhancing reliability and simplifying the design, as shown in Figure 5.9a.

5

Network designs based on standalone repeaters *must* include the cables linking the ring-in/ring-out ports to the repeaters in the calculation. See examples and Figure 5.9b.

Very large rings can use fibre optic cable to interconnect wire centres. Fibre optic cable should also be used for external cable runs where its immunity to electromagnetic interference greatly improves reliability and availability. High security applications and applications that require immunity to electrical noise (e.g. factory automation, process control) should also use fibre optic cable between wire closets.

Fibre repeaters, standalone or integrated into the wire centre(s), offer the same benefits as copper repeaters plus the additional benefits inherent to fibre technology.

5.4   Multiple wiring closet networks with repeaters

Repeaters can be used to extend the maximum size of a non-repeatered ring. A repeater behaves almost the same as a node in that it regenerates the network signal as it passes through. In order to decide where to place repeater units we recommend that you work from a sketch of the overall ring. On this you will place repeaters and perform the calculations until you are satisfied that the configuration has been correctly designed.

For the purpose of calculating the MLL, repeaters allow you to split the ring into segments and to determine the MLL for each segment. The ring is effectively segmented at every repeater because, like an active node, the repeater regenerates the signal. However, unlike an active node it is always in the main ring. Therefore, for planning purposes, every segment can be regarded as a standalone network. If the longest lobe cable in each segment is less than the MLL calculated from the formula *for that segment*, then the whole ring will run with any node active on the ring.

We now have to define our **repeater segment**.

In a network with repeaters, the main ring path will include all cables within the segments plus the cables linking the repeaters. For ease of planning, repeater networks are broken down into smaller segments and the MLL calculated for each segment. A segment is defined as comprising all network components (wire centres, network cables, patch cables and lobe cables) from the repeater connected to the ring-in of the first wire centre in the segment to the associated repeater connected to the ring-out of the last wire centre in the segment. See Figures 5.10a and 5.10b. *A segment does not include the cable between directly connected repeaters.*

In order to calculate the MLL for each segment, the lengths of cables that form part of the main ring path in that segment have to be taken into consideration. The MRL for each segment of a network is called the drive distance. Hence, there will be a drive distance for each segment in your network.

In Token Ring networks using copper repeaters, the drive distance is the sum of the lengths of all Type 1 (or Type 2) cables which form the main ring path for that segment. Note that the drive distance defined above for formula-designed networks is not always the same as that used by IBM in conjunction with their drive distance table(s). It is equivalent to the actual drive distance, as defined in Appendix B, for any active node and is consistent for all repeater segments.

Once we have positioned the repeaters we will be able to calculate the MLL for each segment. So how do we decide where to place our repeaters?

Positioning the repeaters

Repeaters are installed in pairs. One is connected to the ring-out port of (typically) the last MAU in the rack while the other is connected

(a) Integral repeaters

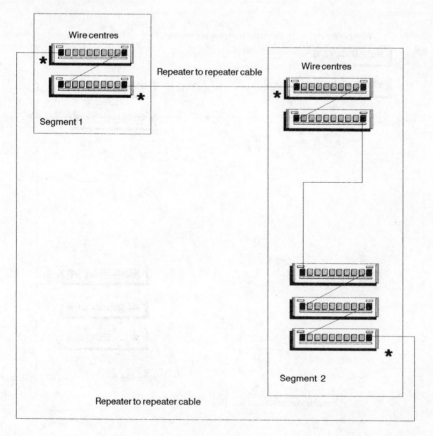

*   Repeater port

Figure 5.10   (a) Repeater segments based on integral repeaters. Repeaters enable
the network to be broken into segments. The MLL can then be calculated for each
segment. Note that for clarity, the patch panels are not shown.

(typically) to the ring-in of the first MAU in the first rack of the next
wiring closet. Both the primary and backup rings should be equipped
with repeaters to ensure the ring continues to operate if a network
cable is disconnected for maintenance or reconfiguration.

Since repeaters are similar to nodes (in introducing jitter), you
must reduce the maximum number of nodes that a single ring can
support by two for each repeater pair being used. This is not a serious
limitation because only very large networks will need several repeater
pairs. For example, on a network with five repeater pairs the maximum number of nodes will be reduced by 10. In most STP network

(b) Standalone repeaters

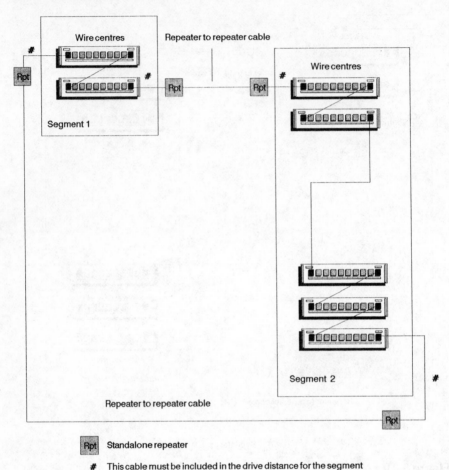

Rpt   Standalone repeater

\#   This cable must be included in the drive distance for the segment

Figure 5.10 *Cont.* (b) Repeater segments based on standalone repeaters. Note that for clarity, the patch panels are not shown.

designs using repeaters, two repeater pairs should normally suffice, unless you have several very long cable runs.

Place the repeater pairs around the longest cable runs between wiring closets. This will ensure that a regenerated signal is transmitted over these long cable runs.

The planning rules can now be extended to incorporate repeaters as follows:

Rule 11   All connections between copper repeaters shall be made with Type 1 (or Type 2) cables.

Rule 12 For networks with copper repeaters, the first repeater pair should be placed around the longest cable run between wiring closets. The second repeater pair should be placed as far away from the first as possible, around a cable run between wiring closets, logically opposite the first pair. Networks with more than two repeater pairs should place the repeater pairs around cable runs between wiring closets such that repeater pairs are equally distant from each other within the practical limitations of the physical network.

Rule 13 All connections between fibre repeaters should use the recommended standard multimode, graded-index fibre of 62.5/125 micron core/cladding diameter. For further details see Chapter 7.

5

The maximum distance between repeater pairs directly connected to each other (no intermediate wire centres) should be available from the manufacturer. Repeaters regenerate the signal in the same way as adapter cards, so repeater–repeater distances for copper cables are normally twice the MCB value. This should, however, be verified with the supplier.

Fibre repeaters, using multimode fibre and LED transmitters, allow distances up to 3 km to be achieved between directly connected repeaters, as discussed in Chapter 7.

With the network designed to conform to rules 1 to 13, we can now replace the MRL term in our general formula with the drive distance for each segment of the network to give Formula C for calculating the MLL. For each segment of a multiple closet network with repeaters, calculate the MLL using Formula C:

Formula C: $MLL_n = MCB - 9*M - 5*C - Dd_n$

where:

MCB : maximum cable budget
M : number of wire centres
C : number of wiring closets
Dd : drive distance for that segment
n : segment number.

Again, all distances are in metres.

If there is more than one rack of wire centres in any wiring closet, in any segment, add ten to the drive distance for every long patch

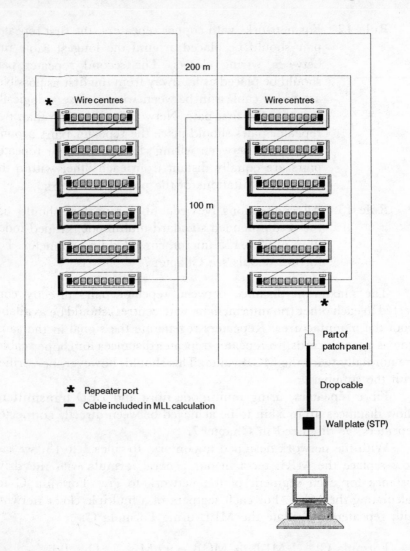

Figure 5.11 Multiple closets with repeaters – use Formula C. Example of a 4 Mbps ring design with one repeater pair and two wiring closets. The MCB is 390 m and the segment drive distance Dd1 is 100 m for a single segment. From Formula C:

$$MLL = 390 - 9 * M - 5 * C - Dd$$
$$= 390 - 108 - 10 - 100 = 172\ m$$

For clarity, the patch panels are not shown.

cable in that segment to allow for long patch cables between racks in the same closet.

The segment number will be chosen by the network designer for planning purposes.

Examples of multiple closet STP network designs with copper repeaters are shown in Figures 5.11 and 5.12. Multiple closet STP (or UTP) network designs with fibre repeaters are considered in Chapter 7.

If the MLL_n for any segment n is less than the longest lobe in that segment, then you must reposition the repeaters, add more repeater pairs following the rules described above, or reduce the distance to the longest lobe as discussed in Section 5.3, until all the lobe lengths are within limits.

5.5 Network design using workgroup wire centres

5

Normally, when we add a wire centre (MAU) or hub to a ring we extend the MRL by the cables connnecting the new wire centre, reducing the MLL by the length of these cables and the equivalent wire centre insertion loss. On the other hand, workgroup wire centres enable us to expand the ring without significantly reducing the MLL because they connect to node cables – not in the main ring path – and are only 'in-ring' when a node is active on the workgroup wire centre. Let us look at how this works.

Workgroup wire centres: operation

The workgroup wire centre (or lobe extender) has a single ring-out port which is connected to the lobe port of any standard wire centre or hub in the main ring. We will call this the host wire centre for the purpose of explanation. There are two possible states: out of ring and in-ring.

In the out of ring state, all nodes connected to the workgroup wire centre will be inactive (i.e. not in the ring); consequently, the relay in the host wire centre lobe port to which it is attached will not be operated. The cable between host and workgroup wire centre, the workgroup wire centre and local node cable will therefore not be con- nected to the main ring.

When any node on the workgroup wire centre joins the ring, the relay in the workgroup wire centre is activated and the join ring signal is extended from the ring-out port of the workgroup to the lobe port

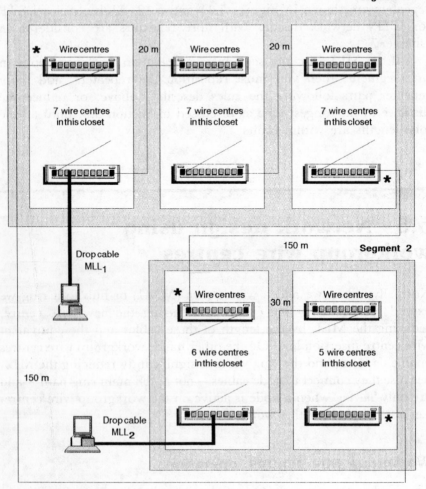

Figure 5.12 Multiple closets with repeaters – use Formula C. Example of a 4 Mbps ring design with two repeater pairs and two wiring closets. At 4 Mbps, the MCB is 390 m; segment 1 has a drive distance of 40 m and segment 2 a drive distance of 30 m.

For segment 1:

$$MLL_1 = 390 - 9 * 21 - 5 * 3 - 40$$
$$= 390 - 189 - 15 - 40 = 146\,m$$

For segment 2:

$$MLL_2 = 390 - 9 * 11 - 5 * 2 - 30$$
$$= 390 - 99 - 10 - 30 = 25\,m$$

Note that patch panels are not shown.

of the attached host wire centre. This, in turn, will join the ring and the workgroup wire centre will now be 'in-ring'.

Workgroup wire centres thus behave like nodes in their connection to their respective host wire centres. The ability of the workgroup wire centre to detach itself from the ring when there are no active nodes means that you can add workgroup wire centres to existing rings without having to redesign the network. Any active node connected to a workgroup wire centre lobe port will repeat the signal (as every other node does) so that, provided the combined length of the workgroup-to-host wire centre connection and workgroup lobe cable does not exceed the previously calculated MLL, no network modification is necessary.

New networks can be designed with workgroup wire centres, using any of the topologies previously described, without having to change any of the design rules or parameters. Another major advantage of workgroup wire centres is that it is possible to save cable for a given topology.

5

The examples in Figures 5.13 and 5.14 illustrate the potential savings in cables for a typical network if workgroup wire centres are used. We can also extend this to UTP designs, and in the following chapters you will see how to use the concept in our sample office network.

The workgroup wire centre concept is also useful in today's modular office since it enables us to move nodes without disturbing the rest of the network.

The design rules can now be extended to incorporate workgroup wire centres as follows:

Rule 14   Workgroup wire centres mounted in racks in wiring closets must be cabled according to the design rules for host wire centres.

Rule 15   For workgroup wire centres mounted in work areas, connections from the wall plate in the work area to the ring-out port of the workgroup wire centre should be made with Type 1 (or Type 2) cable for STP network designs.

Rule 16   For nodes connected directly to the workgroup wire centre lobe ports, use 3 metres, or shorter, Type 6 patch cables.

Rule 17   Connections from the workgroup wire centre lobe ports to secondary wall plates should use Type 1 (or Type 2) cable.

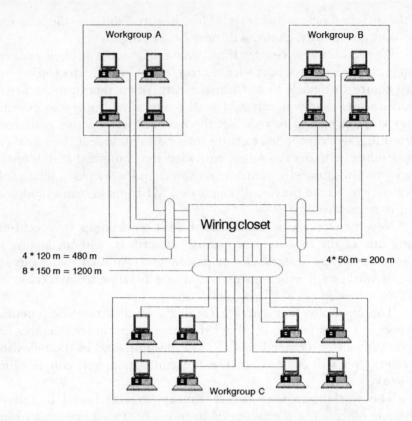

Figure 5.13 Host wire centre design: standard cabling configuration with cables direct to each node. Total length of the main ring cable is 1880 m.

Rule 18   Connections from secondary wall plates in the work area to the nodes can use 3 metres, or shorter, Type 6 patch cables.

Rule 19   Workgroup wire centres *should not* be cascaded to form more than two levels of wire centres, including the host wire centre.

The following steps will enable you readily to design networks using a combination of workgroup and host wire centres.

Step 1   Determine the number and positions of workgroup wire centres as enhancements to existing networks or as part of a new network design, in conformance with Rules 1 to 19.

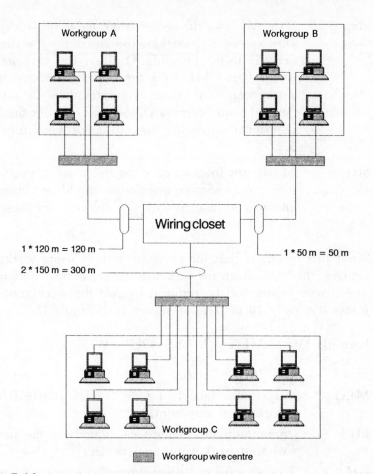

1 * 120 m = 120 m

2 * 150 m = 300 m

1 * 50 m = 50 m

Workgroup wire centre

Figure 5.14   Host/workgroup wire centre design showing the cable savings that can be achieved. In this example, there is one cable for every four nodes, resulting in a total main ring cable length of just 470 m.

Step 2	Calculate the maximum lobe length for the whole network without repeaters or for each segment if you are using repeaters.
Step 3	Ensure that all distances to lobes without workgroup wire centres are less than the MLL by at least 10 metres. If any lobe distances are longer than the MLL, redesign the network according to the design information in previous sections and repeat Step 2 until all lobe distances are less than the MLL.
Step 4	Calculate the MLL for nodes connected to workgroup wire centres by using Formula D below.

Step 5   If the MLL for the nodes connected to the workgroup wire centre is less than (or equal to) the distance derived using Formula D, then the network will work. If the MLL for the nodes connected to the workgroup wire centre is greater than the distance derived from Formula D, then the network should be redesigned using the suggestions detailed in Section 5.4.

Step 6   Maximum lobe lengths for the main network and workgroup wire centre nodes should be checked to ensure compliance with the relevant formulae and Rules 1 to 19.

What this means is that for network designs using workgroup wire centres, the MLL from the host wire centre to any node on the workgroup wire centre will be reduced by just the workgroup wire centre loss (typically 10 metres) as shown in Formula D:

Formula D: $MLG = MLL - GH - WCloss$

where:

MLG   : maximum lobe length for nodes attached to the workgroup wire centre

MLL   : maximum lobe length calculated for the network without workgroup wire centres

GH   : distance from the workgroup wire centre to its connected host wire centre

WCloss   : workgroup wire centre loss expressed as equivalent length of cable.

As before, all distances are in metres.

Note that for networks without repeaters there will only be one value for the MLL. For networks with repeaters, any segment that includes workgroup wire centres *must* use the value of the MLL calculated for that segment.

Workgroup wire centres typically introduce an additional loss of 10 m of cable. For networks where the MLL is at least 10 m less than the maximum, then workgroup wire centres can be added without changing the basic ring design. All network designs should avoid placing nodes at or near the MLL, as stated previously, and should therefore be capable of supporting workgroup wire centres.

Examples of STP network designs using workgroup wire centres are shown in Figures 5.15 to 5.17.

Now that we have seen how the different topologies are made up and how the MLL for each can be calculated from variations of the general formula, we can apply this to any design (from a single segment to a complete network) to verify that it will work, by calculating the MLL and comparing it with the actual lobe distances. Let us do this for the sample office network.

5.6   Calculating the MLL for the sample network

5

The sample office network is based on a multiple wiring closet design without repeaters, so we must use Formula B to calculate the MLL:

Formula B: $MLL = MCB - 9*M - 5*C - ARL$

Assume that we only want to operate at 4 Mbps and the MCB is 390 m. We have: M = 8 wire centres (additional units included for growth), C = 2 wiring closets and ARL = 60 metres. As there is only one rack in each wiring closet, long patch cables do not have to be included in the ARL calculation. Hence:

$$MLL = 390 - 9*8 - 5*2 - 60$$
$$= 390 - 72 - 10 - 60$$
$$= 248 \text{ metres}$$

Examination of the lobe lengths of the sample layout from the cable schedule, the wire centre sequence charts or the site layouts, shows that the maximum node cable length is 60 m.

For the sample office network, the node that is furthest away from a wire centre has a lobe cable length of 60 m. This is well within the maximum lobe length distance calculated above, hence the network design will work.

Whilst we have had to introduce the formula in relation to the different network components and topologies we will meet, and show

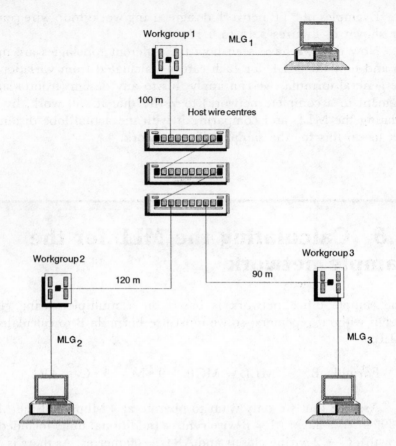

Figure 5.15 Host/workgroup wire centre network design using a single wiring closet. At a data rate of 4 Mbps the MCB is 390 m. Using Formula A for the complete network:

$$MLL = 390 - 9 * 3 - 10 * 0 = 390 - 27 = 363 \text{ m}$$

For Workgroup 1 (Formula D):

$$MLG_1 = 363 - 100 - 10 = 253 \text{ m}$$

For Workgroup 2 (Formula D):

$$MLG_2 = 363 - 120 - 10 = 233 \text{ m}$$

For Workgroup 3 (Formula D):

$$MLG_3 = 363 - 90 - 10 = 263 \text{ m}$$

Note that, for clarity, the patch panels are not shown.

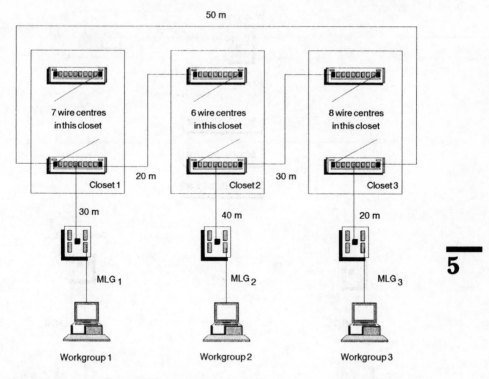

Figure 5.16 Host/workgroup wire centre network design for a multiple closet network. At a data rate of 4 Mbps the MCB is 390 m. Using Formula A to calculate the MLL for the complete network:

$$MLL = 390 - 9 * 21 - 5 * 3 - 80$$
$$= 390 - 189 - 15 - 80 = 106 \text{ m}$$

For Workgroup 1 (Formula D):

$$MLG_1 = 106 - 30 - 10 = 66 \text{ m}$$

For Workgroup 2 (Formula D):

$$MLG_2 = 106 - 40 - 10 = 56 \text{ m}$$

For Workgroup 3 (Formula D):

$$MLG_3 = 106 - 20 - 10 = 76 \text{ m}$$

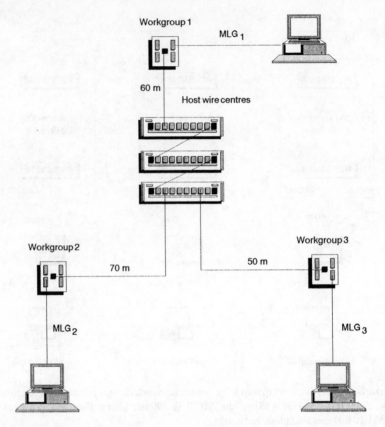

Figure 5.17 Host/workgroup wire centre network design for operation at 16 Mbps using a single closet layout. At 16 Mbps the MCB is 180 m. so using Formula A for the complete network:

$$MLL = 180 - 9 * 3 - 10 * 0 = 180 - 27 = 153 \text{ m}$$

For workgroup 1 (Formula D):

$$MLG_1 = 153 - 60 - 10 = 83 \text{ m}$$

For workgroup 2 (Formula D):

$$MLG_2 = 153 - 70 - 10 = 73 \text{ m}$$

For workgroup 3 (Formula D):

$$MLG_3 = 153 - 50 - 10 = 93 \text{ m}$$

The patch panels are not shown, for clarity.

examples of how it is used, you can see that once we have gone through this exercise the actual verification process is quite simple and quick.

Formulae used in this chapter

Formula A: $MLL = MCB - 9 * M - 10 * L$

Formula B: $MLL = MCB - 9 * M - 5 * C - ARL$

Formula C: $MLL_n = MCB - 9 * M - 5 * C - Dd_n$

Formula D: $MLG = MLL - GH - WCloss$

6

Verifying the design: rules and formulae for UTP cabling

CHAPTER CONTENTS

Chapter summary

Because of the relatively lower cost, lighter weight and greater flexibility of UTP cable compared with STP cable, UTP is often the 'cable of choice' in installations adopting a structured cabling system. UTP cable can also be terminated with telephone-type RJ45 connectors, making it easier to install and test than systems using the STP/MIC cable/connector alternative. For these reasons, UTP cabling systems are being used in preference to STP (and even coax) cabling systems as the copper cable of choice in today's local area networks. Chapter 6 shows how we can design Token Ring networks based on UTP cable in the same way, based on the same topologies and using the same formulae as for STP rings.

The two major new considerations we must be aware of in designing UTP cable networks are:

(1)   near end crosstalk (NEXT), that is, the amount of transmitted signal that 'leaks' into the receiver pair at the adapter

(2)   increased attenuation of UTP vs STP cable.

These combine to reduce the maximum overall distance for node connections to the ring.

We show how these factors affect the maximum lobe length and how the same basic formulae can be used to design complete UTP rings or UTP segments of larger rings. Hence the concepts and rules introduced in the previous chapter are expanded to enable the reader to design UTP networks. The basic considerations remain the same, ensuring consistency in the Token Ring network design across both STP and UTP cabling systems. The rules can therefore be extended to other types of cabling and, in particular, to fibre optic cables as discussed in the next chapter.

After considering the single closet and multiple closet topologies, with examples, we look at the advantages of the workgroup wire centre concept to the network designer. Finally we use the sample office layout to illustrate the use of UTP for the ring network with three different topologies.

6

6.1   Introduction

In this chapter we will show you how to verify the design – Step 5 in the design stages – for your network, or segments of your network, utilizing unshielded twisted pair (UTP) cabling. As we consider the different network topologies, we will follow a similar sequence to that used in Chapter 5 showing how the formulae are used to verify our designs by enabling us to calculate the maximum lobe length of our network.

Examples of network designs operating at 4 and 16 Mbps are included for:

• single wiring closet topology   (Section 6.2)

- multiple wiring closet topology without
  repeaters   (Section 6.3)
- multiple wiring closet topology with
  repeaters   (Section 6.4)
- network design using workgroup wire
  centres   (Section 6.5).

Although UTP cable can be used in Token Ring networks in almost the same way as STP cable, we do have to consider the differences between the two types of cable and how they affect our designs. We first look at the importance of the quality of the signal in relation to UTP cable and then go on to consider the main factors that can affect the reliability and integrity of the data. We can then take these effects into consideration as we define the planning rules for UTP structured cabling systems, in the same way as we did for STP systems in the previous chapter. We can then develop the formula we will use to verify our UTP network designs.

6.1.1 Signal quality

Signal quality is very important in determining the maximum cable budget (and hence MLL) when the transmit and receive pairs in the cable are not shielded from each other, as they are in STP cable. The quality of the signal on the ring is determined by the cable characteristics which, in turn, vary as a function of the data rate. We must, therefore, use the right quality (grade) of UTP cable to enable us to build reasonably sized networks that will be reliable, error free and cost-effective.

Several types of existing UTP cables have been tested and new types manufactured to ensure that MLLs of up to 85 m can be achieved at 16 Mbps using MAUs and NICs from a range of suppliers. These are often referred to as data grade UTP cables and, as shown in Appendix A, are classified into various levels – level 1 being the lowest grade and level 5 the highest – primarily according to the maximum data rate they can reliably support.

Let us take this a little further by briefly looking at the four main areas where UTP cable systems differ from STP cable systems:

- effects of the transmitted signal power,
- level of signal distortion or jitter,

- characteristic impedance of the cable,
- the physical connectors.

Transmitted power

On unshielded cable there is a limit to the maximum power that can be transmitted into the cable because as the transmit power is increased the level of the signal induced in the adjacent receive pair increases. This is called **near end crosstalk** (NEXT); unless there is at least 30 dB isolation (from transmit to receive pairs) then interference and errors can result.

Level 4 UTP cable (see Appendix A), designed for carrying data, will have a NEXT separation of 40 dB or better. Ring designs supporting up to 100 nodes and MLLs up to 100 m can be readily achieved using this grade of cable.

Signal distortion (jitter)

The two major forms of jitter are overshoot jitter and pattern dependent jitter. Both reduce the maximum number of nodes that can be attached to rings at 16 Mbps and the corresponding MLLs. New designs of interface circuits using filters to reduce overshoot jitter and retiming circuits to reduce pattern dependent jitter have been – and continue to be – developed to minimize or eliminate unwanted jitter. This is often referred to as active UTP technology.

It is possible to use this active filtering technology to reduce the levels of crosstalk and the effects of jitter. This enables greater distances to be supported over the lower grades of cable and is particularly attractive if someone needs to run (Ethernet or Token Ring) over existing level 3 cable. With improved jitter reduction we can also support more nodes on a given ring – potentially up to the full specification of the IEEE 802.5 recommendations. However, this technology is more expensive than passive filtering with a consequent increase in the price of the card or hub module.

Active UTP support is the subject of ongoing standards discussions to ensure interoperability between equipment from different manufacturers. Once finalized, the technology should enable us to build large (up to 260 nodes) UTP networks at 16 Mbps with lobe lengths up to 150 m, albeit at a slightly higher initial cost.

There is little difference between designing the network using active or passive filtering components and then verifying the design using the appropriate formulae. The design steps, planning rules and basic formulae will be similar and the principles will be the same. The differences will be in the maximum number of nodes that can be supported on a single ring and the value for the maximum cable budget. These factors will be supplied by the manufacturer in the normal way.

Note that although the IEEE 802.5 recommendations allow some 260 nodes as the maximum per ring, for ease of maintenance and network management it is often advisable to limit this to 100.

Cable characteristics and physical connectors

In order to use UTP effectively, the cable characteristics have to be matched to the interface card and wire centre. Several manufacturers supply cards with on-board RJ45 connectors for UTP. Cards that only have STP (D-type) connectors can be attached to UTP networks via a small, external media filter. This filter removes the higher order harmonics from the signal (to limit the VHF radiation from UTP systems to acceptable, and usually mandatory, levels), and provides a nominal 100 ohms characteristic impedance to match that of the cable. The characteristic impedance for STP cable is 150 ohms.

Several manufacturers also supply MAUs and hubs that support direct UTP connection (via RJ45 ports) and active or passive filtering technology. Hubs with only STP (MIC) connectors can be fitted with MIC to RJ45 adapters.

6.1.2 UTP network designs

In the same way as for STP networks, the factors that affect the MLL for UTP designs include:

- number of MAUs (wire centres)
- number of wiring closets
- main ring path length.

Hence the design principles discussed earlier, together with those considerations applicable to UTP cables, will enable us to design and verify UTP Token Ring networks.

The same design formulae can be used for UTP planning by reducing the maximum cable budget to reflect the shorter distance capabilities of UTP cable. The formulae method for planning Token Ring networks is particularly attractive because it can be used for different network speeds, media types and wire centre platforms simply by changing the relevant parameters. This gives a consistent and easy-to-use approach to network design.

The design rules and formulae we derived for STP networks can now be extended and used to design and verify UTP networks by enabling us to calculate the MLL for a given topology. The cable budgets will be different for UTP designs than for STP designs as a result of the smaller drive distances available with UTP cable and these are reflected in the UTP-based formulae.

Let us look at the general formula again and see how we can adopt this to verify UTP designs.

6.1.3 General formula

The derivation of the general formula is included in Appendix B. This formula allows us to calculate the MLL for our network or segment from a knowledge of the maximum cable budget and the respective component losses:

$$MLL = MCB - K1 * M - K2 * C - MRL$$

where:

MLL	:	maximum lobe length
MCB	:	maximum cable budget
K1, K2	:	constants
M	:	number of MAUs
C	:	number of wiring closets
MRL	:	main ring path length.

The maximum cable budget is a function of the signal drive capability of the adapter card and is provided by the manufacturer. For further details see Appendix B. The MRL is the sum of all the lengths of cable that make up the main ring (i.e. *not* including node cables).

The general formula can be simplified for UTP-based Token Ring networks and segments by applying the following recommendations in your design. This will ensure that the predictable losses, which can affect the cable budget and MLL in structured cabling

6

systems, are taken into consideration wherever possible. The network designer then only has to consider the site-dependent drop cable lengths – the MLL from the formula, as shown in the examples.

Note that some of the parameters referred to in the recommendations can be reduced (e.g. patch cable lengths), to increase the maximum lobe length. Take care to ensure that any changes to the recommendations are valid (e.g. from manufacturer's data) and that they reflect the actual installation, otherwise it could result in incorrect network designs. Some parameters cannot be changed as these are fixed by physical or electrical limitations.

All references to UTP cable infers conformance to the parameters and specifications of Belden AWG-24 cable. Cables of a higher specification (e.g. AT&T type 1061 and 2061) have better crosstalk and frequency characteristics resulting in improved transmission capabilities. Systimax™ cables 1061/2061 will realize at least the distances calculated by the UTP formulae illustrated in this guide.

Table 6.1   Token Ring planning rules for single ring UTP designs.

Rule 1	The maximum number of nodes supported is 260. The actual number will depend on the level of jitter reduction incorporated in the manufacturer's products. One hundred nodes (with twelve or thirteen 8-node MAUs) is considered a practical maximum for most UTP rings.
Rule 2	The maximum number of wire centres is 33 (but see note for Rule 1).
Rule 3	The maximum number of wire centres per rack is 12.
Rule 4	Within a rack, connect wire centres to each other with 1 metre, or shorter, UTP data cables.
Rule 5	Connect wire centre lobe ports to the distribution panel within a rack with 3 metre, or shorter, UTP data cables.
Rule 6	Use only one level of patching per lobe cable.
Rule 7	Patch cables/connectors should have a total insertion loss at 16 Mbps of less than 1 dB and a crosstalk better than -35 dB.
Rule 8	NEXT at the network interface card with UTP cable connected must be better than -35 dB.
Rule 9	Connect wire centres in different racks within the same wiring closet with 10 metre, or shorter, UTP data cables.
Rule 10	Connection from the distribution (patch) panel to the wall plate in the work area should use approved data grade UTP cable.
Rule 11	Connections from the wall plate in the work area to the node adapter can use 3 metre, or shorter, UTP data cables.

By adopting these recommendations, the network installation will conform to recognized high standards. The general formula then becomes:

$$MLL = MCB - 5M - 5C - MRL$$

where:

K1   :   5 (assumes 1 m patch cable plus 8-node MAU insertion loss equivalent to 4 m of UTP cable)

K2   :   5 (length of cable equivalent to the connector loss between two wiring closets).

Before we consider the various network topologies, let us look at how we physically cable MAUs (or hubs) in a UTP environment. In the same way as for STP-based hubs and MAUs, the ring-in and ring-out ports on UTP systems are used to connect MAUs together for increased node capacity. The ring-out of the 'last' MAU is connected to the ring-in of the 'first' MAU to realize a closed, physical ring.

An alternative configuration is possible when loopback switches are included on the ring-in/ring-out ports of MAUs with RJ45 connectors or, if using IBM type MAUs with UTP adapters, the ring-in/ring-out ports are left unconnected (i.e. the IEEE 802.5 connector is in automatic loopback). Note that RJ45 connectors do not automatically loop the transmit to receive signal paths when disconnected as do IEEE 802.5 connectors.

In this configuration the last wire centre is not connected back to the first, as shown in Figure 6.1.

Configuring the network with the data looped back at the first and last wire centres and providing loopback switches has the following advantages:

- live data is always present on the standby ring
- wire centres can be added without having to remove cables
- any wire centre or group of wire centres can be isolated without having to disconnect cables
- requires less cable
- simpler network design.

Leaving out this cable will not affect the operation of the network. Rather, the formulae can take account of the different main

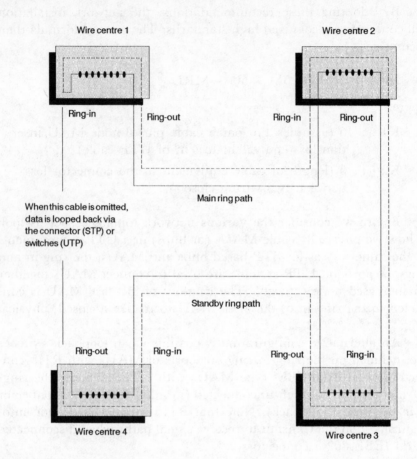

Figure 6.1 Wiring topology usually adopted on UTP systems. In such networks the cable from the last ring-out port back to the first ring-in port is often omitted, as shown here.

ring path cable lengths using the MRL variable, as we shall see in the examples.

6.2 Single wiring closet networks without repeaters

Single closet UTP designs are the most often used configurations because they are easier to plan and give the maximum lobe distances.

Single closet designs, however, can give rise to a higher total cable length (the sum of all the cables to each node), as we have seen, but this is offset by the lower costs associated with UTP systems and can be reduced further by using workgroup wire centres, as described in Section 6.5.

Note that for all token ring networks the design should avoid placing nodes at distances aproaching the MLL as this will limit the future expansion capabilities of your network. It is better to site wire centres closer to the work areas, thus having two or more wiring closets, and to keep drop lengths shorter, if you expect your network to grow.

With the UTP network (or segment) designed to conform with Rules 1 to 11, we can then calculate the MLL for a single closet network design using Formula A:

Formula A: $MLL = MCB - 5 * M - 10 * L$

where:

MCB : maximum cable budget
M   : number of wire centres (MAUs)
L   : number of long patch cables.

6

All distance are in metres, as previously.

In Formula A the main ring path length (MRL) is the length of all long cables linking wire centres between racks, as shown in the example in Figure 6.4. If the size of the network requires only a single rack, often the case when hubs or concentrators are used, then Formula A reduces to:

$MLL = MCB - 5 * M$

Examples of typical, single rack configurations are shown in Figures 6.2 and 6.3.

Use the value for MCB equivalent to the cable and wire centre type you will be using on your network. Typical values for level 3 data grade UTP cable are shown in Table 6.2.

Table 6.2 Maximum cable budgets for level 3 UTP designs.

Data rate	MCB
4 Mbps	200 m
16 Mbps	120 m

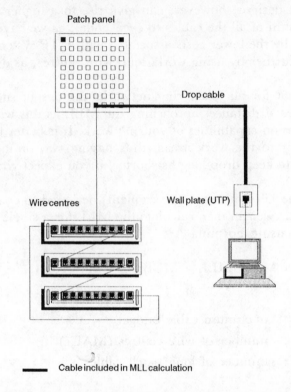

Patch panel

Drop cable

Wire centres

Wall plate (UTP)

━━━ Cable included in MLL calculation

Figure 6.2 Single wiring closet UTP network design operating at 4 Mbps using level 3 data grade cable. At 4 Mbps the MCB is 200 m. Using Formula A:

$$MLL = 200 - 5 * M - 10 * L$$
$$= 200 - 15 - 0 = 185 \text{ m}$$

If the maximum lobe length from the above calculation is less than the longest node in your network, it may be possible to redesign the network to use multiple wiring closets (with or without repeaters) or workgroup wire centres to place wire centres closer to the work areas. Although single wiring closet networks are easier to design and manage than multiple closet networks, there may be applications where multiple closets will be required. Hence we will now consider designs based on two (or more) wiring closets connected either directly or by repeaters. As we shall see, as a result of the lower MCB of UTP cable, copper-based repeaters are rarely used in UTP configurations. Fibre optic repeaters are most often used in conjunction with UTP designs, as discussed in Chapter 7.

In Section 6.4 we will look at some of the advantages of network designs based on a combination of UTP and fibre media; we discuss how to configure networks with fibre optic repeaters in Chapter 7.

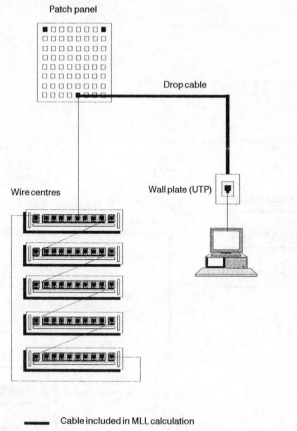

Cable included in MLL calculation

Figure 6.3 Single wiring closet UTP network design operating at 16 Mbps using level 3 data grade cable. At 16 Mbps the MCB is 120 m. Using Formula A:

$$\text{MLL} = 120 - 5 * M - 10 * L$$
$$= 120 - 25 - 0 = 95\,\text{m}$$

6.3   Multiple wiring closet networks without repeaters

In order to design and plan networks with more than one wiring closet, in addition to the number of wire centres (or hubs) we will need to know:

- number of wiring closets
- length of the main ring path (backbone).

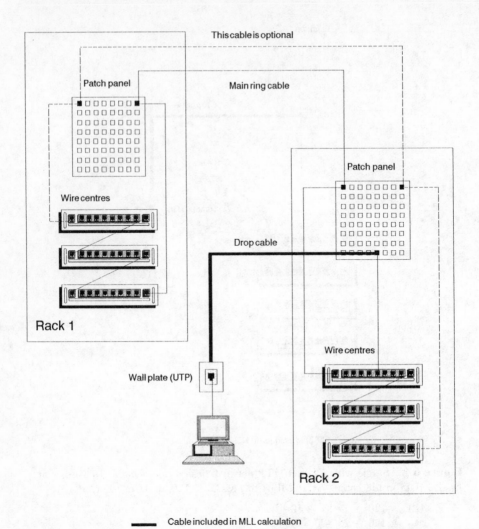

Figure 6.4 Single wiring closet UTP network design with two racks operating at 16 Mbps using level 3 data grade cable. At 16 Mbps the MCB is 120 m. Using Formula A:

$$MLL = 120 - 5 * M - 10 * L$$
$$= 120 - 30 - 10 = 80 \text{ m}$$

We will be able to calculate the maximum lobe length as before. If the calculated MLL is greater than the length of the longest lobe cable in your network it will function without repeaters. However, if the MLL determined by using Formula B, below, is less than the longest lobe length in your network then you will have to use repeaters or redesign the network by resiting the wiring closets or using workgroup wire centres. If it is not possible to resite the wiring closets, fibre optic repeaters can be used between closets.

Note that a work area can be connected to the ring using host wire centres that are not contained in a rack or in a wiring closet. In these cases, for planning purposes each work area containing one or more host wire centres should be treated as if it were an additional wiring closet.

Standalone MAUs and hubs can be incorporated into the planning process by adding the following two rules:

Rule 12   Host wire centres installed in a work area should be connected to each other with 1 metre UTP data cables.

Rule 13   All connections between wiring closets and from wiring closets to/from host wire centres in work areas should be made with UTP data cable.

Determining the MRL in multiple wiring closet designs   6

In multiple wiring closet networks we have to consider the lengths of cable interconnecting wiring closets and work areas if these contain additional host wire centres. Most UTP network designs do not connect the last wire centre back to the first wire centre; in this case the length of cables connecting the wiring closets is the main ring path length (MRL). Note that if the last wire centre is connected back to the first wire centre then the value for MRL in Formula B should be replaced by the adjusted ring length (ARL) as defined in Chapter 5.

With the network designed to conform to Rules 1 to 13, the MLL for multiple closet networks without repeaters can be calculated using Formula B:

Formula B: $MLL = MCB - 5 * M - 5 * C - MRL$

where

MCB   :   maximum cable budget
M   :   number of wire centres
C   :   number of wiring closets
MRL   :   main ring path length.

All distances are in metres. If there is more than one rack of wire centres or hubs in a closet then add 10 to the MRL for every long

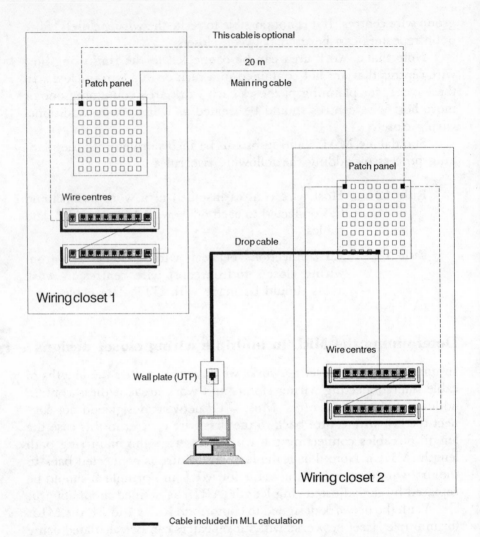

Figure 6.5 Multiple wiring closet UTP network design operating at 16 Mbps using level 3 data grade cable. At 16 Mbps the MCB is 120 m. Using Formula B:

$$\text{MLL} = 120 - 5 * \text{M} - 5 * \text{C} - \text{MRL}$$
$$= 120 - 20 - 10 - 20 = 70 \, \text{m}$$

patch cable in the network to allow for long patch cables between racks in the same closet.

Examples of multiple closet UTP network designs without repeaters are shown in Figures 6.5 and 6.6. Note that in multiple wiring closet designs, wherever possible the closets should be sited close to work areas to keep lobe cables short. This gives greater flexibility, is easier to expand and assists maintenance.

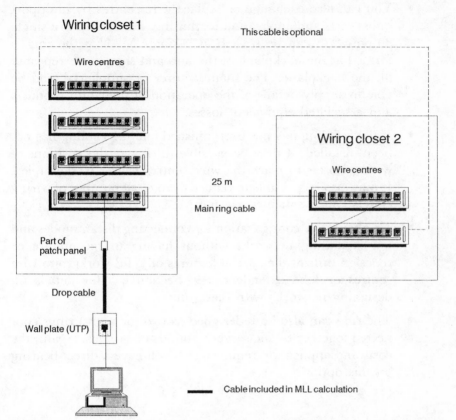

Figure 6.6 Multiple wiring closet UTP network design operating at 16 Mbps using level 3 data grade cable. At 16 Mbps the MCB is 120 m. Using Formula B:

$$MLL = 120 - 5 * M - 5 * C - MRL$$
$$= 120 - 30 - 10 - 25 = 55 \text{ m}$$

Patch panels not shown for clarity.

If the MLL from the above calculation is less than the longest node in your network, it may be possible to redesign the network to avoid using fibre optic repeaters. Some suggestions are given below. If you decide to use fibre repeaters then you must use the rules and formulae detailed in Chapter 7:

- If the calculated MLL is less than the length of the longest node cable in your network it may be possible to extend the MLL by reducing the number of wire centres in the ring, especially if additional wire centres have been included in the initial calculation to allow for growth.

- You can also exchange or replace wire centres by multiport hubs, costs and application permitting. For example, a single 80-port hub can be treated as a single MAU if the ring is formed at the backplane of the hub and signals are repeated on the backplane. The manufacturer or supplier should be able to supply details of the operation of their hub products and associated equivalent losses.

- If the building has not been finished and the cabling has not been installed, it may be possible to change the positions of wiring closets to place the wire centres nearer to the nodes. It may also be possible to reduce the overall number of wiring closets which can increase the MLL.

- An alternative configuration for connecting distant nodes and for expanding networks without having to reconfigure or redesign utilizes the special features of UTP workgroup wire centres or lobe extenders. See Section 6.5 for details on designing networks with these units.

- The ring can also be redesigned as two (or more) rings connected together by file servers, routers or bridges. Again, the costs and application requirements will have a direct bearing on this option.

Repeaters

The maximum cable budgets for UTP networks designed with level 4/5 grade UTP cable are typically 250 m at 4 Mbps and 150 m at 16 Mbps. Even with these higher values, compared with level 3 grade cable, in multiple wiring closet configurations without repeaters it is difficult to maintain reasonable lobe lengths as the MLL is reduced by the length of cable interconnecting the wiring closets (the main ring path).

At 4 Mbps the maximum cable budget may be large enough to enable us to design multiple closet networks with reasonable distances between closets and still have 50 to 100 m for the lobe length. However, at 16 Mbps in all but the simplest designs (two closets less than 50 m apart) the main ring path length will reduce the MLL below a useful distance (less than 20 m).

Ring size can be increased by using copper or fibre optic repeaters. The latter are preferred because the additional distance achievable from copper UTP repeaters is still not that attractive when compared with the filtering required, maintenance implications and additional cost. For a similar outlay we can use fibre with its many advantages.

Fibre optic cable should always be used for external cable runs where its immunity to induced electromagnetic interference greatly improves reliability and availability. High security applications and applications that require immunity to electrical noise (e.g. factory automation, process control) should also use fibre optic cable between wire centres.

Note that if a network is designed for 4 Mbps operation today but will be upgraded to 16 Mbps in future, the placement of wire centres and wiring closets and the MLL calculations should be based on 16 Mbps cable budgets. A combination of fibre for the main ring path and UTP for the node connections is particularly attractive because it accommodates almost all applications at 4 and 16 Mbps without having to redesign or modify the network.

6

6.4   Multiple wiring closet networks with repeaters

Whilst most manufacturers offer fibre repeaters for UTP (as well as for STP) designs, few offer copper repeaters. However, if you *are* designing networks, or segments of networks, using UTP copper repeaters then they should conform to the same design rules as for STP with copper repeaters, as described in Section 5.4, or UTP with fibre optic repeaters, as described in Chapter 7.

As you can see, Formula C is the same. The difference will be in the distance between the UTP copper repeaters. Inter-repeater distances for UTP copper repeaters will be supplied by the manufacturer. Typical distances are of the order of 350 m only.

Let us consider some of the advantages of ring designs based on a mixture of fibre and UTP media.

Maximum lobe lengths/simplified design

When multiple wiring closets are connected by fibre, each closet can be treated as a single closet for the purpose of design and verification because the cable between closets (fibre) is effectively isolated by the repeaters and hence does not reduce the MLL. See Figure 6.7.

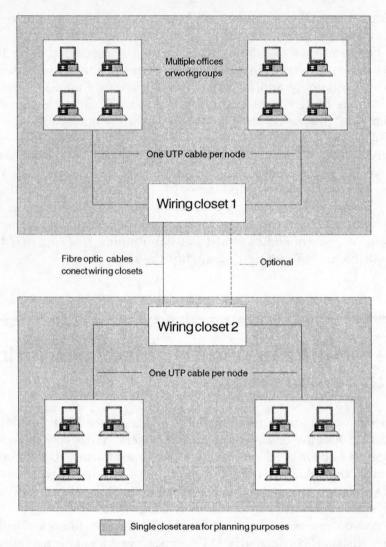

Figure 6.7 Multiple wiring closet network showing how the closets can be connected by fibre optic cable. The 'return' cable linking the first and last MAUs can be omitted.

Office blocks and campus sites

A popular choice for high-rise buildings or campus sites is to use fibre as the backbone and UTP for the horizontal (floor) runs. This combination is very flexible (providing a backbone with all the advantages of fibre and node connections with the inherent advantages of UTP) in terms of capital cost, installation and ongoing maintenance.

The fibre backbone has, perhaps, a higher initial capital cost, but provides a high performance upgradable service (100 Mbps FDDI: Fibre Distributed Data Interface) and the cost associated with connecting multiple nodes over a large area is optimized.

Mixing UTP and STP cable on the same ring

As we have seen, UTP and STP cable have different characteristics. The two major factors that have to be considered if we want to have a single ring with STP and UTP segments are the different impedances and the fact that UTP cable will radiate if the signal is unfiltered.

The mismatch in impedance will give rise to attenuation differences as the signal passes from one cable to the other which can affect the design and reliability of the network as well as making it more difficult to plan. Radiation could affect equipment near the UTP cables, which may or may not be serious, but, more importantly, almost always contravenes local mandatory limits. Hence it is advisable to try to design rings using either all UTP or all STP cable for the copper media.

If you have to use UTP and STP segments on the same ring, then either:

- Adopt a concentrator or hub that enables you to mix STP and UTP modules connected via the backplane. This avoids the impedance mismatch and usually incorporates filtering of the signal between modules. Do not join modules via front-panel ring-in/ring-out ports from STP to UTP as you will still be mixing STP/UTP directly.

or

- Use fibre optic repeaters between the STP and UTP segments of your ring. The fibre effectively isolates the segments of the ring and the filtering and impedance matching is done within the repeaters.

For the hub topology, use the UTP planning rules and formula for the whole ring (i.e. worst case), unless the manufacturer can recommend otherwise. For the fibre repeater topology you can use the STP rules and formula for the STP segment(s) and the UTP planning rules and formula for the UTP segment(s).

6.5   Network design using workgroup wire centres

Token Ring UTP workgroup wire centres: operation

The UTP workgroup wire centre (or lobe extender) concept is identical to the STP workgroup wire centre concept and has similar advantages:

- wire centres can be placed close to workgroups
- does not form part of the main ring path lengths
- is not in-ring when no nodes are active on the workgroup wire centre
- reduces the total amount of cable.

The workgroup wire centre appears as a node on the host wire centre to which it is connected. For a given number of nodes, if they are all connected to workgroup wire centres then this will reduce the total number of host wire centres required. As each host wire centre reduces the MLL by the wire centre loss and the patch cable length, the fewer host wire centres in the main ring the greater the possible lobe lengths. For example, if we want to build a ring of 96 nodes at 16 Mbps, based on the standard 8-node MAU, with the ability to support lobe lengths of (say) 100 m, then we can do so, with minimal planning, using workgroup wire centres. This is because the number, and hence equivalent cable loss, of host wire centres needed to support 96 nodes is less.

We can design new networks with workgroup wire centres, based on any of the topologies previously described, or incorporate them into existing networks, without having to change the design, as long as the lobe lengths are not already at their maximum. We shall use the sample office network to show how this can be achieved, in addition to the other examples included in this chapter.

The UTP workgroup wire centre concept is especially useful in today's modular office since it can be relocated easily without disturbing the rest of the network. Workgroup wire centres on UTP networks produce a similar reduction in main ring path cable lengths as for STP network designs, as illustrated in the comparison between Figures 5.13 and 5.14.

We can now extend the Token Ring planning rules to include support for UTP Workgroup wire centre support as follows:

Rule 14   Workgroup wire centres must be cabled with the same data grade UTP cable as for host wire centres.

Rule 15   For workgroup wire centres mounted in the same closets as their associated host wire centres, the remote port must be connected directly to the host lobe port (i.e. not via a patch cable). Connections from the lobe ports of the workgroup wire centre must be cabled in the same way as lobe ports of host wire centres.

Rule 16   For workgroup wire centres mounted near their associated nodes, the cable from the host wire centre in a wiring closet to the workgroup remote port will be configured as a normal node cable.

Rule 17   Connections from the workgroup wire centre lobe ports to secondary wall plates must use UTP data cable.

Rule 18   Connections from secondary wall plates in the work area to the nodes must use 3 metre, or shorter, UTP data cables.

Rule 19   Workgroup wire centres should not be cascaded to form more than two levels of wire centres, including the host wire centre.

The following steps will enable you readily to design networks using a combination of workgroup and host wire centres:

Step 1   Determine the number and positions of workgroup wire centres as enhancements to existing networks or as part of a new network design, in conformance with Rules 1 to 19.

Step 2   Calculate the maximum lobe length for the whole network without repeaters or for each segment if you are using repeaters.

Step 3   Ensure that all distances to lobes without workgroup wire centres are less than the MLL by at least 10 metres. If any lobe distances are longer than the MLL, redesign the network according to the design information in previous sections and repeat Step 2 until all lobe distances are less than the MLL.

Step 4   Calculate the MLL for nodes connected to workgroup wire centres by using Formula D below.

Step 5   If the MLL for the nodes connected to the workgroup wire centre is less than (or equal to) the distance derived using Formula D, then the network will work. If the MLL for the nodes connected to the workgroup wire centre is greater than the distance derived from Formula D, then the network should be redesigned using the suggestions previously outlined.

Step 6   Maximum lobe lengths for the main network and workgroup wire centre nodes should be checked to ensure compliance with the relevant formulae and Rules 1 to 19.

This means that for network designs with workgroup wire centres, the MLL from the host MAU (or hub) to any node will be reduced by the workgroup wire centre loss, as compared with the direct connection, typically by 10 m. The MLL for nodes attached to the workgroup wire centre (MLG) is therefore simply expressed using Formula D:

Formula D: MLG = MLL – GH – WCloss

where

MLG   :   maximum lobe length for nodes attached to the workgroup wire centre

MLL   :   maximum lobe length calculated for the network without workgroup wire centres

GH   :   distance from the workgroup wire centre to its connected host wire centre

WCloss   :   workgroup wire centre loss expressed as equivalent length of cable.

All distances are in metres.

For networks without repeaters there will only be one value for the MLL. For networks with repeaters, any segment that includes workgroup wire centres *must* use the value of the MLL calculated for that segment.

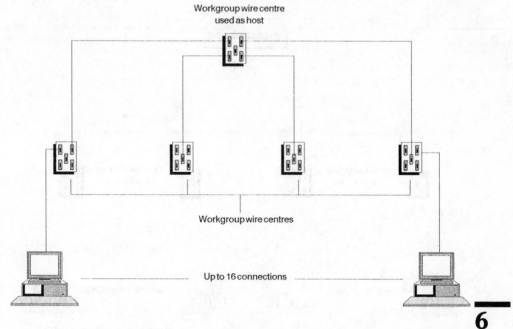

Figure 6.8 Workgroup wire centre design for up to 16 nodes. Workgroup wire centres (MAUs) can be used for new designs or as extensions to existing networks. At 16 Mbps the MCB is 120 m. Using Formula A for the complete network:

$$MLL = 120 - 5 * M - 10 * L$$
$$= 120 - 5 = 115 \text{ m}$$

Hence for workgroup MAU, using Formula D:

$$MLG = MLL - GH - 10 = 105 - GH$$

Node to host distance $= MLG + GH = 105$ m

Workgroup wire centres introduce a typical additional loss of 10 m. For networks where the MLL is at least 10 m less than the maximum, workgroup wire centres can be added without changing the basic ring design. All network designs should avoid placing nodes at or near the maximum lobe length, as stated previously, and will therefore be capable of supporting workgroup wire centres.

Networks with up to 16 nodes per ring can be very cost-effectively designed with UTP cable and 4-node workgroup wire centres that support a master–slave configuration. Figure 6.8 illustrates how a 4-node workgroup wire centre can be used in host mode to support up to four further workgroup wire centres and provide connectivity to 16 users. Networks with up to 32 nodes per ring can also be

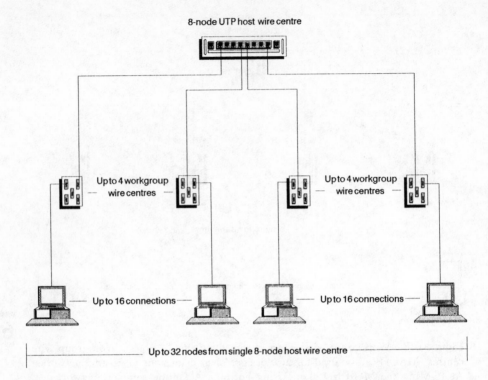

Figure 6.9   Host/workgroup wire centre design for up to 32 nodes at a data rate of 16 Mbps. The MCB is 120 m at this data rate, so using Formula A for the complete network:

$$MLL = 120 - 5 * M - 10 * L$$
$$= 120 - 5 = 115 \, m$$

Hence for a workgroup operating at 16 Mbps, using Formula D:

$$MLG = MLL - GH - 10 = 105 - GH$$

Node to host distance = MLG + GH = 105 m

configured cost-effectively with UTP cable and a combination of an 8-node host wire centre and up to eight 4-node workgroup wire centres, as shown in Figure 6.9.

This concept can be extended to multinode concentrators enabling a single, central concentrator equipped with (say) 25 nodes to support a 100-workstation ring. The workstations connect to 4-node workgroup wire centres placed at or near the respective users. We can design even larger rings by using any correctly configured combination of host and workgroup wire centres. Workgroup wire centres and directly attached nodes can be mixed in any combination on host

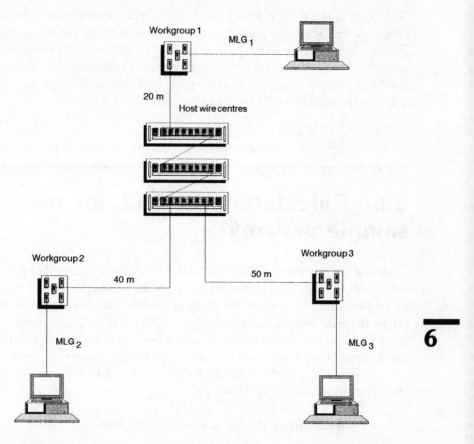

Figure 6.10 Host/workgroup wire centre network design. At a data rate of 16 Mbps, the MCB is 120 m, so using Formula A for the complete network:

$$MLL = 120 - 5 * 3 - 10 * 0$$
$$= 120 - 15 = 105 \text{ m}$$

For workgroup 1 (Formula D):

$$MLG_1 = 105 - 20 - 10 = 75 \text{ m}$$

For workgroup 2 (Formula D):

$$MLG_2 = 105 - 40 - 10 = 55 \text{ m}$$

For workgroup 3 (Formula D):

$$MLG_3 = 105 - 50 - 10 = 45 \text{ m}$$

wire centres, hubs and concentrators up to the maximum recommended for a single ring.

Examples of UTP network designs using workgroup wire centres are shown in Figures 6.8 to 6.10.

Now that we have seen how the different topologies are made up and how the MLL for each can be calculated from variations of the general formula, we can apply this to any design (from a single segment to a complete network) to verify that it will work by calculating the MLL and comparing it with the actual lobe distances. Let us do this for the sample office network.

6.6   Calculating the MLL for the sample network

If we use the same multiple wiring closet topology for our UTP design as we did for our STP design then, from Formula B, we can see that at 4 Mbps our MLL would be 90 m and at 16 Mbps it would be 10 m, without using repeaters. The longest lobe cable is 60 m so we either have to redesign the network or add fibre optic repeaters to support the longest lobe if we want to run at 16 Mbps now or in the future.

We can look at three UTP designs that will enable us to support the 60 m lobe length at 16 Mbps:

- single wiring closet, host wire centre design
- single wiring closet, host/workgroup wire centre design
- multiple closet with repeaters design.

6.6.1   Single wiring closet, host wire centre design

As shown in Figure 6.11, the sample network can be designed with a single, central wiring closet positioned at the corner of area H. The longest lobe cable, from new cable schedules or sequence charts, is now 70 m. We can now calculate the MLL for the sample office network using Formula A for single closet network designs:

Formula A: MLL = MCB − 5 * M − 10 L

assuming 16 Mbps operation with UTP wire centres.

For 39 nodes we require a minimum of five 8-node wire centres, hence:

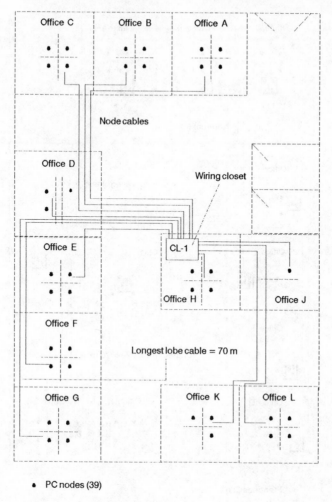

Figure 6.11 Single wiring closet design for the sample office network.

MLL = 120 − 25 = 95 m

This is longer than the maximum lobe distance for the sample network, so the network design will work.

6.6.2 Single wiring closet, host/workgroup wire centre design

As shown in Figure 6.12, the sample network can be designed with a single, central wiring closet positioned at the corner of area H and workgroup wire centres located in each work area A, B, C, etc. The

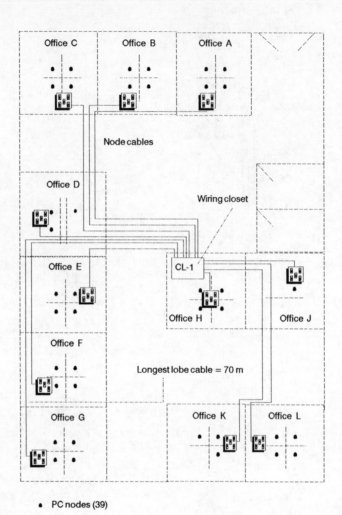

Figure 6.12 Host/workgroup wire centre design for the sample office using a single wiring closet and workgroup wire centres (MAUs).

longest lobe cable, from new cable schedules or sequence charts, is now 70 m.

We can calculate the MLL for the sample office network using Formula A for single closet network designs:

Formula A: MLL = MCB − 5 M − 10 L

assuming 16 Mbps operation with UTP wire centres.

For 39 nodes we require ten 4-node UTP workgroup wire centres and two 8-node host wire centres. The MLL for the whole network will therefore be:

MLL = 120 – 10 = 110 m

The maximum lobe length for the network with workgroup wire centres will be the MLL for the host wire centre design minus the workgroup wire centre loss of 10 m. Therefore, the maximum lobe length possible in this design is 100 m. As this is longer than the maximum lobe distance for the sample network, the network design will work. In addition, up to six more 4-node UTP workgroup wire centres can be added (24 nodes) without having to recalculate the MLL.

6.6.3   Multiple wiring closet with fibre repeaters

As shown in Figure 6.13, the sample network can be designed with multiple wiring closets connected by fibre optic repeaters. This enables us to treat each closet as a single closet network, for the purpose of design, and will give the maximum lobe distances. We can now calculate the MLL for each segment using Formula A for each wiring closet. (Formula C reduces to Formula A in this case.)

6

Segment 1:
Formula A: MLL = MCB – 5 M – 10 L

assuming 16 Mbps operation with UTP wire centres.
For 27 nodes we require four wire centres, hence:

MLL = 120 – 20 = 100 m

This is longer than the maximum lobe distance of 60 m for Segment 1 of the sample network so the network design will work.

Segment 2:
Formula A: MLL = MCB – 5 M – 10 L

assuming 16 Mbps operation with UTP wire centres.
For 12 nodes we require two wire centres, hence:

MLL = 120 – 10 = 110 m

This is longer than the maximum lobe distance of 20 m for Segment 2 of the sample network so the network design will work.
Again you can see that whilst we have had to spend some time looking at the differences between STP and UTP cabling systems,

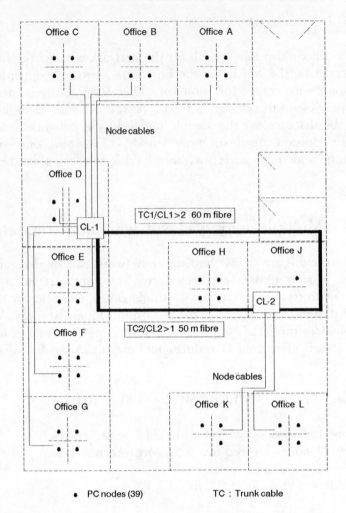

Figure 6.13 Sample office network using two wiring closets linked by fibre optic cable.

if the design rules are followed and the corresponding value for the maximum cable budget is known, then we can quickly verify our design.

In the next chapter we look at the characteristics of fibre which make it ideal for use in Token Ring networks, and see how fibre optic repeaters can be used to extend the length of the backbone cable and hence the physical size of the ring.

Formulae used in this chapter

Formula A: $MLL = MCB = 5 * M - 10 * L$
Formula B: $MLL = MCB - 5 * M - 5 * C - MRL$
Formula D: $MLG = MLL - GH - WCloss$

7

Verifying the design: rules and formulae for fibre optic cabling

CHAPTER CONTENTS

Chapter summary

In previous chapters we looked at network design based on shielded and unshielded twisted pair cabling. These concepts are extended, in this chapter, to include the use of fibre optic cable for part or the whole of your network. The chapter first highlights the main properties of optical fibre and then shows why multimode fibre is the most commonly used medium for local area networks. Further details of other fibre technologies are included in Appendix A.

The chapter continues by showing how the formulae developed for designing STP and UTP networks can be applied to networks where part or all of the networks will use fibre. From this it will be seen that networks with an 'all fibre' backbone are simple to design and provide a great deal of flexibility, particularly with respect to the lengths of node cables.

Whilst fibre to the node may be required for certain applications (e.g. banking, defence), a typical use of fibre is to connect individual wire centres, concentrators or hubs to each other to form a fibre-cabled ring or fibre backbone. Copper cable (either UTP or STP) is then used from the hub to the node. This topology is discussed in this chapter and typical designs are considered.

When you have finished and understood this and the preceding chapters you will be very familiar with most aspects of Token Ring design. Whilst in planning networks based on specific vendors' equipment there may be certain characteristics that you will have to consider, on the whole, you will be able to design most networks using the information you have now learned.

7.1   Introduction

In this chapter we first review the overall properties of fibre optic cable (fibre) and how it is used in Token Ring networks, then we look at the types of fibre links and show how Formula C is used to verify our design.

As we saw in Chapter 1, in a ring topology data is transmitted from one active user to the next via the node cable and associated ports on the MAU, or wire centre, to which they are attached. Similarly, MAUs (wire centres) or hubs are interconnected by cabling from the respective ring-out of one unit to the ring-in of the following unit by a direct point-to-point link.

7

Fibre cable is ideal for point-to-point links and hence is a popular choice for backbone connections in a Token Ring network, that is, for the interconnections between wire centres and/or wiring closets. Less popular, but experiencing a growing demand, are fibre-based connections to nodes. Direct fibre to node support will depend on the application – typically where high security is required – and costs.

In terms of network planning, any node connected by fibre can be treated as a separate segment, as the fibre repeater effectively isolates each node port, so the MRL for the copper-based segments is not affected.

The MLL for fibre to the node connections will be 2 to 3 km depending on the type of fibre and the ring data rate. (See Appendix A.)

Copper repeaters enable the main ring path to be extended for larger, single ring applications. Fibre repeaters enable even larger rings to be implemented (for example, campus type applications) and provide greater configuration flexibility on both STP and UTP rings, as we saw in Chapter 6 for the sample office network. This is due to the inherent properties of fibre which include:

- immunity to induced electrical noise
- no electrical radiation
- isolation
- small size and low weight
- up to 3 km between repeaters.

Immunity to induced electrical signals

Data is transmitted along the fibre as short pulses of light. Because the transmission medium is fibre, electrical signals and noise do not cause any induced effect within the cable.

No electrical radiation

Data transmission is not electrical via copper cable so power is not emitted at radio frequencies. The light pulses are kept within the cable by the cladding and an external sleeve, ensuring that no light is radiated.

Isolation

There is no electrical connection between two points linked by fibre. This means that loop currents can be prevented and installations at different potentials can be safely connected together. This is particularly advantageous in isolating earth potential differences and is one of the main reasons why fibre is strongly recommended for connections between buildings and for linking systems that have separate mains power supplies.

Fibre should always be used for external data cabling because of its inherent immunity to lightning and other potentially serious high voltage sources.

Small size and low weight

Shielded and unshielded copper cables have a larger diameter than the equivalent capacity fibre cable. Their small size makes fibre cables very attractive in applications were space is at a premium, particularly in applications where the existing ducts may be full or nearly full.

Installation and commissioning costs can also be lower, especially if recent developments in fibre technology are adopted for splicing, terminating and laying the cables. A relatively new technique for fibre installation is known as blown fibre because it enables long lengths of fibre to be 'blown' into tubes (using compressed air) quickly, efficiently and without damage to the fibres.

The inherently low weight of fibre makes it a good choice in applications where the heavier copper is more expensive to fix and support. Typical examples are vertical risers in tall office buildings and where cable is laid on overhead racking.

7.2   Types of fibre optic link

As we have seen, networks based on Token Ring technology pass data round the ring in one direction in a point-to-point manner. Consequently, it is inherently straightforward in terms of design and implementation to support a unidirectional medium like fibre.

Bus topologies which rely on a broadcast type of transmission can utilize fibre with special electronics but are more suited to a bidirectional medium such as copper (e.g. coax cable).

7

Fibre links can be installed today to run at 4 Mbps and can be upgraded to 16 Mbps operation without reducing the inter-repeater distances. This means that you do not have to redesign the network as you increase the data rate. Similarly it is possible to upgrade to even higher speeds (100 Mbps FDDI) over the same fibre with the same inter-repeater distances. Within the limits of the bandwidth of the cable, drive distances are reasonably constant and 2 to 3 km between repeaters is possible from 4 to 100 Mbps, depending on the quality of fibre used.

Fibre can be used almost anywhere in a Token Ring network, including for lobe cables and patch cables, but is most often used for part or all of the main ring path. Some manufacturers incorporate fibre repeaters within the corresponding wire centres or concentrator hubs, thus saving cable and improving reliability, as discussed earlier.

In many cases the advantages of fibre cable, both in initial implementation and ongoing network maintenance, can easily justify the slightly higher capital costs. Sometimes the hidden costs associated with copper cable (e.g. installing new ducts) can make the overall project more expensive than a fibre alternative.

Details of the typical fibre used on 4 and 16 Mbps Token Rings, together with the main fibre characteristics, are given in Appendix A.

Note that fibre repeaters are configured in pairs and monitor the status of the link at all times. Fibre repeaters from different manufacturers may not be compatible and should not, therefore, be connected together over the same fibre.

7.3   Verifying fibre optic network designs

In terms of planning your network with fibre repeaters, the design steps, concepts and considerations are identical to those we used for copper repeaters. All we need to know is the maximum distance between repeaters, which will depend on the type of fibre used, transmitter power and receiver sensitivity (as detailed in Appendix A). We can then again verify our designs using Formula C.

Fibre repeaters will segment the ring in the same way as copper repeaters and we can calculate the MLL for each segment in exactly the same way as we did for the multiple closet designs with (copper) repeaters in Chapter 5.

Note that fibre and copper repeater segments can be freely mixed on the same ring provided matching copper or fibre repeater pairs are used at each end of the cable(s) between closets, in the normal way.

For multiple closet designs in which any two wiring closets are linked by fibre, Formula C will enable us to calculate the MLL for the corresponding segment. Expressing Formula C in its general format we have:

Formula C: $MLL = MCB - K_1 * M - K_2 * C - Dd$

where:

K_1 : wire centre/cable insertion loss
K_2 : wiring closet insertion loss

A ring may span several floors of an office complex and need to be externally linked to a second building. Copper repeaters can be used within one, or both, buildings and fibre repeaters used to connect the building networks together, as shown in Figure 7.1.

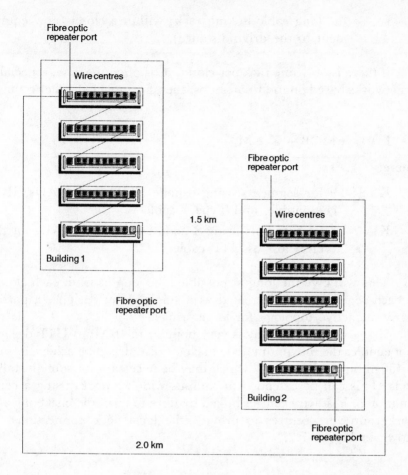

Figure 7.1 Multiple closet network design using fibre repeaters and fibre optic cable to connect two racks in different buildings. The repeaters are integral to the wire centres.

Whilst fibre and/or copper repeaters enable us to design rings to suit almost any application requirement and physical topology, a popular configuration is to build a fibre backbone by linking all wiring closets using fibre repeaters. This topology gives rise to segments which (typically) contain only a single wiring closet. As well as utilizing the advantages of fibre this makes them very easy to verify. In these designs Formula C reduces to:

$$MLL = MCB - K_1 * M - 10 * L$$

where:

L : the long cable linking racks within a closet (now equivalent to the drive distance).

If there is only one rack per closet, as is often the case, especially in networks based on multiport hubs, then Formula C further reduces to:

$$MLL = MCB - K_1 * M$$

where:

K1 : 9 for segments using 8-node STP-based MAUs, IBM compatible, and Type 1 cable

K1 : 5 for segments using 8-node UTP-based MAUs for the typical loss of UTP cable.

This will give the longest possible lobe lengths from each closet, as each segment can be treated as a single closet design – a particularly attractive topology for larger rings.

Using fibre in this way is very popular in 16 Mbps UTP designs as it enables the maximum node to closet distance to be achieved – up to 150 m on level 5 cable – which may be necessary for some installations. This can be extended to campus wide networks using a combination of host wire centres linked by fibre to form the backbone and workgroup wire centres to provide the local node connections, as shown in Figure 7.2.

7.3.1 Calculating MLL values within a fibre optic segment

We can now look at examples of general purpose multiple closet networks with closets linked by fibre repeaters and calculate the MLL to verify the designs in the usual way. When fibre repeaters are used to extend the maximum main ring size of the network, or to provide electrical isolation, then the ring can be segmented, for planning purposes, at the fibre repeaters in exactly the same way as for copper repeater networks. See Figure 7.3. The MLL for each segment is calculated in the same way as for copper repeaters using Formula C.

We can now extend the Token Ring planning rules to include support for fibre repeater pairs:

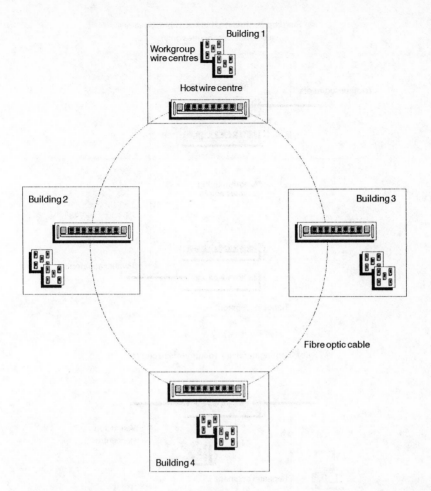

Figure 7.2 Multiple closet design options with fibre repeaters, showing how a 'campus' network can be built using fibre optic cable to connect the MAUs in the wiring closet in each building, thus forming a fibre backbone.

Rule 20   The MLL value within a segment bounded by fibre repeaters is calculated in the same way as for a segment bounded by copper repeaters and the same rules apply.

With the network designed to conform to Rules 1 to 20, the MLL for each segment of the multiple closet network with fibre repeaters is calculated using Formula C:

Formula C: $MLL_n = MCB - K1 * M - 5 * C - Dd_n$

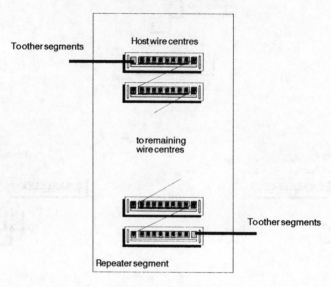

(a) Ring segment defined between fibre repeaters
(using host wire centres only)

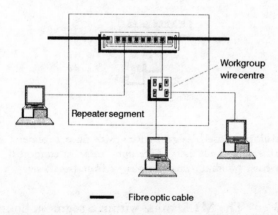

(b) Ring segment with workgroup wire centres

——— Fibre optic cable

Figure 7.3 Multiple closet design options based on fibre repeaters: (a) Ring segment defined between fibre repeaters (host wire centres only), and (b) Ring segment with workgroup wire centres. Fibre repeaters segment the ring like copper repeaters and the segments are defined in the same way.

where:

MCB : maximum cable budget
K1   : wire centre loss
M   : number of wire centres

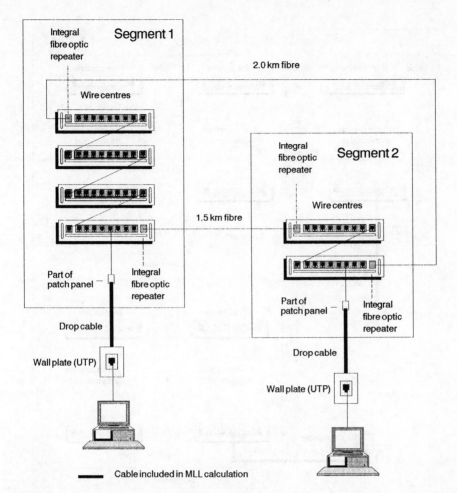

Figure 7.4 Multiple closet 16 Mbps UTP network design based on level 3 data grade cable and fibre repeaters between closets. At 16 Mbps the MCB is 120 m; the drive distance for both segments is zero. Using Formula C:

For segment 1, $MLL_1 = 120 - 5*4 = 100$ m
For segment 2, $MLL_2 = 120 - 5*2 = 110$ m.

C	:	the number of wiring closets
Dd	:	drive distance for that segment
n	:	the segment number.

All distances are in metres, as previously.

If there is more than one rack of wire centres or hubs in a closet then add 10 to the MRL for every long patch cable in the network to allow for long patch cables between racks in the same closet.

7

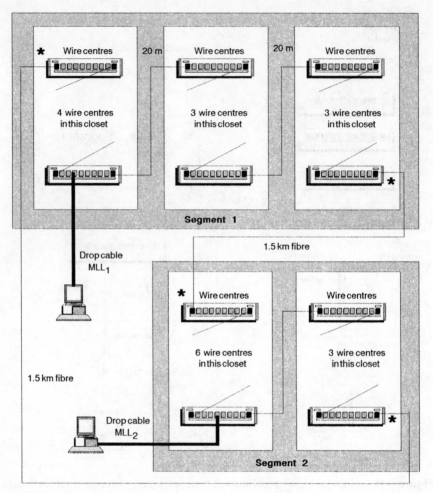

★   Fibre optic repeater port
━   Cable included in MLL calculation

Figure 7.5 Multiple closet 16 Mbps network design based on STP (Type 1) cable with fibre repeaters between distant closets. At a data rate of 16 Mbps, the MCB is 180 m. The drive distance is 40 m for segment 1 and 30 m for segment 2. Using Formula C:

For segment 1, $\text{MLL}_1 = 180 - 9*10 - 5*3 - 40 = 35$ m
For segment 2, $\text{MLL}_2 = 180 - 9*8 - 5*2 - 30 = 68$ m.

The segment number will be chosen by the network designer for planning purposes. The value for K1 will depend on the wire centre type (STP/UTP):

K1 : 9 for STP segment (assuming 3 m patch cords and 6 m equivalent cable loss)

K1 : 5 for UTP segment (assuming 1 m patch cords and 4 m equivalent cable loss).

Examples of general purpose multiple closet network designs with fibre repeaters are shown in Figures 7.4 and 7.5. If MLL_n for any segment (n) is less than the longest lobe in that segment then you can reposition the repeaters, add more repeater pairs following the rules described above, or reduce the distance to the longest lobe, as discussed in Chapter 5.3, until all lobe lengths are within limits.

Let us now summarize what we have learned about designing Token Ring networks and then go on to the last stages in the planning process by looking at how we do the cost analysis and finalize the network plan. We will discuss these last two steps in Chapter 8.

8

Summary and final planning steps

CHAPTER CONTENTS

Chapter summary

In this final chapter we summarize what we have considered in the previous chapters. A simple design verification technique is outlined and we show you how you can use approximate equipment costs to check on the validity of your design from the standpoint of *do I have enough equipment for this network to work?* Too much or too little and the costs will quickly highlight this.

As we have tried to show, network design comes down to an iterative process of positioning components to suit the overall criteria. You then successively modify your design, according to the rules, until the criteria have been satisfied as closely as possible. Once you have mastered the basic concepts introduced and discussed in this book, you will be able to design Token Ring networks easily and quickly with the confidence that you know that when they are installed they will work.

Good designing!

8.1   Introduction

In Chapter 1 we saw how Token Rings work and what factors we had to consider, unique to ring topologies, to begin to design our networks. We also looked at the logical versus physical ring and how wire centres, MAUs, hubs and concentrators are used to connect nodes to the network. We then went on to look at the planning process in Chapter 2 by considering the components that make up a Token Ring, the node interface cards (NICs), MAUs (and their interconnection), repeaters and the media. The differences between structured and non-structured cabling systems were discussed and from this we were able to define seven planning steps:

(1)   determine the location of present and (if possible) of future nodes,

(2)   determine the location of wiring closets and wire centres,

(3)   determine the media requirements,

(4)   determine the repeater requirements,

(5)   verify the network design,

(6)   perform the cost analysis,

(7)   finalize the network plan.

In order to show you how to design Token Ring networks based on structured cabling systems (typical for planned and permanent installations) we went through the planning steps in some detail. From these we saw that once the principles and formulae are known and you have practised with a few designs of your own, then it becomes fairly straightforward to plan Token Ring networks and the designs can be verified quite quickly.

These first few chapters gave us all the information needed to plan Token Ring networks. From this, we can plan networks with a high degree of confidence since the rules and guidelines that we have discussed allow us to verify our designs before they are implemented.

In Chapters 5, 6 and 7, respectively, we showed you how to verify your design for STP cabling, UTP cabling and fibre optic cabling, whether one type of cable is used on the whole ring or whether different cable is used for separate segments.

8

We can now do a cost analysis of the major components that we have chosen in our design to see if the capital costs are reasonable and within expected ranges. If they are we can then finalize the plan by ensuring that all the documentation and forms are complete, that all lobe lengths are within limits and that the design rules have been followed throughout. This can either be done by the designer or design team or can be given to an independent third party.

8.2   Cost analysis

Because of the wide variation in component prices and as prices will change with time (usually downward thanks to competitive market forces), it would be misleading to analyse capital costs by using current prices. Hence we will illustrate the principle by standardizing the node interface card cost and using this as a comparison for the other major components in the network.

We would like to have a quick, but probably fairly rough, measurement of network costs; we can obtain this from a knowledge of the equipment capital costs used in our network. Installation, commissioning and associated costs cannot be quantified easily and the best price is almost always obtained by competitive quotation.

We will therefore look at how we can get a 'feel' for whether the capital equipment costs are reasonable. The best way to do this is to compare the quoted prices against typical costs. What can we use as our yardstick for the typical costs? The most popular is that of the typical cost per node. From this we can quickly determine expected costs by multiplying the cost per node by the number of nodes in our network. We can then compare it with the actual equipment costs to see if it is reasonable.

Determining the minimum costs per node

Node interface card

Assuming an NIC costs one hundred units, we can determine the absolute minimum cost per node, which we can then use as our datum point, by adding to this the cost per port of an 8-node MAU and the equivalent connection cost which represents the cumulative costs of cables, racks, patch panels etc.

MAUs (wire centres)

Whilst hubs and multinode concentrators allow us to connect more nodes per wire centre, the variation in prices from manufacturer to manufacturer and the different capacities make it difficult to use them for cost comparisons. The standard (IBM compatible), non-intelligent 8-node MAU, however, maintains a reasonably stable cost versus functionality which we can use to arrive at our cost per node.

Based on an NIC cost of 100, an 8-node MAU will normally be 200 units or less. Hence the cost per port will be 25 units (200/8).

Connection costs

The connection costs will include the costs of:

- adapter cable,
- office wall plate,
- drop cable (cable from wall plate to patch panel),
- proportion of patch panel costs equivalent to one node,
- rack price (PSUs, etc.) divided by the number of nodes in a rack,
- patch cable from patch panel to MAU port,
- proportion of MAU ring-in/ring-out patch cables.

8

All of these costs can be identified except for the cost of the drop cable as this is, in effect, the MLL we calculate when verifying the designs. We have therefore assumed a mean length of 70 m for the drop cable which will cater for over 90% of all installations. Based on this length, the typical cost per port for the connection components will be 25 units. Hence the minimum cost per node for comparison purposes is 150 units (100 for the NIC, 25 per port for the MAU and 25 per port for cabling, etc.).

Note that hubs and concentrators become cost-effective in larger networks. For small networks (typically less than 50 nodes) the start up costs of the hub chassis, power supplies, control or management modules increase the effective cost per port. In some cases this can double or triple the cost per node for small installations (e.g. 30 nodes or less).

Many users, especially those with corporate networks where the design must allow for growth, invest in hubs knowing that after 30 nodes, say, the cost per port starts to approach those based on an 8-node MAU design, and after 50 nodes starts to fall below this figure.

The size of the present and proposed installation, as well as its functionality and management, will dictate whether multinode hubs are deployed. However, the very fact that we can calculate a cost per node based on the traditional 8-node MAU can be used as a yardstick, for measuring not only the cost-effectiveness of networks using 8-node MAUs, but also the cost-effectiveness of the hubs themselves!

We can now multiply the cost per node (150 units) by the number of nodes in our network to obtain an indication of whether the capital costs are reasonable and to determine whether we have either left something out or put in too much equipment – overprovisioned on node ports, for example.

If an NIC costs £400, the typical cost per node would be £600 for a structured cabling system. If you had a 40-node network you would expect capital costs of the order of £24,000. Naturally a two-closet network design for a 40-node ring would be more expensive than a single closet solution, and this can be easily taken into account.

The objective of this simple cost analysis approach is that, in our example, if our capital equipment cost was £10,000 we would recognize that we had a good bargain or question the quality or quantity of components in our design. Conversely, if it costs £60,000 then we might want to check again because it looks, at first sight, somewhat expensive. It may, for example, be an all-fibre network, in which case the cost analysis should take this into account.

By applying sensible and current average prices to the key elements of equipment used in our Token Rings it is possible to get an indication of whether our network designs are cost-effective and reasonably priced.

8.3 Finalizing the network plan

In order to finalize the network plan, all aspects of the design should be documented and checked off either by the designer, another member of the design team or an independent consultant. This usually involves ensuring that:

- all drawings are available and complete,
- all nodes are clearly positioned and marked,
- all lobe lengths have been checked and verified to be within the MLL for your topology and cabling systems and, where possible, have allowed for future growth,
- all schedules are up to date,
- all equipment lists, with prices, have been completed.

In short, all the information that is needed to be able to hand over the procurement and, if necessary, proceed with installation and commissioning, is documented and available.

The most important aspect of finalizing the plan is to ensure that the maximum lobe lengths are within the limits recommended by the supplier and/or manufacturer, as explained in this book. The design should also be checked for conformance with the planning rules, as applicable to your topology and segments, and prevailing standards for the network, the installation (safety, radiation etc.) and any other local laws or regulations. Once this has been done you can feel confident that not only will your network work, but will run error free for the designed lifetime, meeting the full local and international standards and performance expected of today's LANs.

APPENDIX A

Copper and fibre optic cables

It is very important to ensure the highest quality for the supply, installation and testing of the cable plant for all types of network. The media (and associated connectors) form the major backbone of your networks and, by design, carry all the data. If the media are incorrectly specified or installed, or the network badly designed, then data may not be carried reliably.

IEEE 802.5 networks can be designed to run over the three major types of cabling systems in use today, including shielded twisted pair (e.g. IBM Type 1), unshielded twisted pair (e.g. AT&T Systimax 1061/2061) and fibre optic (e.g. ODC 62.5/125 STII).

The following data is provided as a basic reference to the types of cable that can be used on IEEE 802.5 networks. For more detailed information you will need to contact the manufacturers or suppliers of the required cable. This will include details on impedance, attenuation and crosstalk similar to those shown in the twisted pair level definitions of Figure A.1, which quantifies data cable characteristics into five levels:

Level 1 cable is designed for ordinary telephone service at frequencies up to 20 kHz.

Level 2 cable is designed to support data transmission up to 4 Mbps.

Level 3 cable is designed to support data transmission up to 16 Mbps.

Level 4 cable is designed to support data transmission up to 20 Mbps.

Level 5 cable (IBM Type 1 STP) is designed to support data transmission up to 100 Mbps.

	AWG	Shield	Data rate (Mbps)	Characteristic impedance (Ohms)	Maximum attenuation (dB/Km)	Mutual capacitance (pF/m)	Near end crosstalk dB (min)
Level 1	22/24	None	<1	N/A		N/A	N/A
Level 2 IBM Type 3	22/24	Optional	4 max	90-120 @ 256kHz	13.2 @ 256 kHz	N/A	N/A
				87-117.5 @ 512kHz	18.7 @ 512 kHz		
				85-114 @ 772KHz	22.2 @ 772 kHz		
				84-113 @ 1MHz	27.1 @ 1 MHz		
				Type 3 Media only	26.4 @ 1 MHz		
Level 3 EIA-SP1907	24	Optional	16 max	100 ± 15 @ 1 MHz	25.7 @ 1 MHz	60 max	43 @ 772 kHz
				100 ± 15 @ 4 MHz	52.8 @ 4 MHz		32 @ 4 MHz
				100 ± 15 @ 10 MHz	99.0 @ 10 MHz		26 @ 10 MHz
				100 ± 15 @ 16 MHz	132 @ 16 MHz		23 @ 16 MHz
Level 4 Extended distance	24	Optional	20 max	100 ± 15 @ 1 MHz	19.8 @ 1 MHz	42 max	40 @ 12-20 Mhz
				100 ± 15 @ 4 MHz	39.6 @ 4 MHz		53 @ 3-5 MHz
				100 ± 15 @ 10 MHz	66.0 @ 10 MHz		
				100 ± 15 @ 16 MHz	82.5 @ 16 MHz		
100 Ohm IBM DGM	22	Optional	16 max	100 ± 15 @ 1 MHz	16.5 @ 1 MHz	42 max	40 @ 12-20 Mhz
				100 ± 15 @ 4 MHz	39.6 @ 4 MHz		53 @ 3-5 MHz
				100 ± 15 @ 10 MHz	52.8 @ 10 MHz		
				100 ± 15 @ 16 MHz	66.0 @ 16 MHz		
Level 5 IBM DGMs	22	Individual and braid	20 - 100	150 ± 10 @ 3-20 MHz	10.6 @ 1 MHz	27 max	40 @ 12-20 Mhz
					22.1 @ 4 MHz		58 @ 3-5 MHz
					35.0 @ 10 MHz		
					45.2 @ 16 MHz		

Figure A.1 Cable characteristics: level definitions. All conductors are solid.

A.1 Copper cables

A.1.1 ETL verification program

This program is operated by ETL Testing Labs of Cortland NY, USA. It is intended to offer a consistent set of test procedures for a range of independent cable manufacturers. Under the program, sample reels of cable are selected periodically and randomly from the participant's production lines or stock and are tested and inspected by ETL for their conformity to specified standards, such as IBM or AT&T. Inspections and tests are referenced for performance requirements against the cabling system specifications of the respective Standards Authority. This is usually the major manufacturer's standard. When the samples of cable under test meet the specified levels then the entire production of that manufacturer is authorized to bear the ETL mark and is listed in the ETL Program Directory.

For further information please contact ETL at:

ETL Testing Labs Inc.
Rt 11, Industrial Park
PO Box 2040
Cortland NY 13045
Attn Electrical Division

A.1.2 Cable types

Cable:	Type 1 Non plenum data cable (indoor)
ETL spec:	4716748
Description:	Two twisted pairs of 22 AWG solid conductors for data communications, each pair enclosed in a braided cable shield and the whole covered in a metal sheath. For indoor use, not fire resistant.
Cable:	Type 1 Non plenum data cable (outdoor)
ETL spec:	4716734
Description:	Two twisted pairs of 22 AWG solid conductors for data communications enclosed in a corrugated, metallic cable shield with appropriate sheath. Type 1 outdoor cable is suitable for aerial installation and for permanent placement in underground conduits.
Cable:	Type 1 Plenum data cable (indoor)
ETL spec:	4716749
Description:	Two twisted pairs of 22 AWG solid conductors for data communications, each pair enclosed in a braided cable shield and the whole covered in a metal sheath. For indoor use, fire resistant.

Cable: Type 2 Data with telephone cable (indoor)
ETL spec: 4716739
Description: Two twisted pairs of 22 AWG solid conductors for data com-
                munications, each pair enclosed in a braided cable shield and
                the whole covered in a metal sheath. Also included inside the
                cable jacket are four additional pairs of 22 AWG solid con-
                ductors for use on telephone circuits.
                For indoor use, not fire resistant.

Cable: Type 2 Data with telephone cable (plenum)
ETL spec: 4716738
Description: Two twisted pairs of 22 AWG solid conductors for data com-
                munications, each pair enclosed in a braided cable shield and
                the whole covered in a metal sheath. Also included inside the
                cable jacket are four additional pairs of 22 AWG solid con-
                ductors for use on telephone circuits.
                For indoor use, fire resistant.

Cable: Type 6 Patch panel data cable
ETL spec: 4716743
Description: Two twisted pairs of 26 AWG stranded conductors for data
                communications, enclosed in braided shield with appropriate
                sheath.
                For indoor use, not fire resistant.

Cable: Type 8 Data cable
ETL spec: 4716750
Description: Four flat, parallel 26 AWG solid conductors for data commu-
                nications, shielded with copper foil and of flat cross-sectional
                construction.
                For indoor use under carpets, etc., not fire resistant.

Cable: Type 9 Plenum data cable
ETL spec: 6339583
Description: Two twisted pairs of 26 AWG solid, or stranded, conductors
                for data communications, enclosed in a braided cable shield
                covered with an appropriate sheath.
                For indoor use, fire resistant.

Cable: Type 3 Data cable
ANSI spec: ANSI/ICEA S-80-576-1983
Description: Two twisted pairs of 22 AWG or 24 AWG solid conductors
                for data communications, enclosed in an appropriate sheath.
                For indoor use, not fire resistant.
                Equivalent specifications include REA PE-71, AT&T
                DIW-4/24, Bell System 48007.

Cable: Systimax
AT&T spec: 1061
Description: Multi-pair twisted cable of 24 AWG solid conductors for data
                communications, with a minimum 30 twists/metre, enclosed
                in an appropriate sheath.
                For indoor use, not fire resistant.

Cable: Systimax
AT&T spec: 2061
Description: Multi-pair twisted cable of 24 AWG solid conductors for data

communications, with a minimum 30 twists/metre, enclosed in an appropriate sheath.
For indoor use, fire resistant.

Cable: Systimax
AT&T spec: 1261
Description: Multi-pair twisted cable of 24 AWG solid conductors for data communications, with a minimum 30 twists/metre and overall shield, enclosed in an appropriate sheath.
                For indoor use, not fire resistant.

Cable: Systimax
AT&T spec: 2261
Description: Multi-pair twisted cable of 24 AWG solid conductors for data communications, with a minimum 30 twists/metre and overall shield, enclosed in an appropriate sheath.
                For indoor use, fire resistant.

Note that networks designed to run on Systimax cables should use 4-pair cable.

Each vendor has its own in-house code for the various cable types available. However, they will normally accept the manufacturer's part number as a reference. IBM have a wide range of cables for LAN and general data communications applications, but other manufacturers supply cables to ETL, ANSI and related standards. These include AMP, AT&T, Belden, BICC, Montrose, Pirelli, NEK, SIECOR, STC and Sumitomo.

A.1.3 Cable parameters for UTP Token Rings

Token Ring networks can support 16 Mbps operation over UTP cable if the cable parameters are equal to or better than the following:

Conductor size	22 or 24 AWG
Number of pairs	2, 3 or 4 maximum
Characteristic impedance	84 to 113 ohms at 1 MHz
Mutual capacitance	29 pF/m or less
Attenuation	27 dB/km at 1 MHz or less
DC resistance	95 ohms/km nominal
NEXT	−35 dB or better
Twist ratio	Minimum 8 twists per metre

(The twist ratio is critical to error free operation at higher data rates. Higher twist ratios give improved transmission and can lead to increased distance capabilities. UTP cables with twist ratios of 20 and 30 twists per metre are available.)

Level 4 and 5 UTP cables are suitable for use on 16 Mbps Token Rings systems. Level 3 UTP cable may be suitable for use at 16 Mbps if it is good quality and pairs are selected from tests that yield the required level of NEXT separation.

Category 3, 4 and 5 cable specifications are defined by ANSI as described in the ANSI/EIA/TIA 568-1991 standard. Category 3 and 4 cable specifications are almost identical to the level 3 and 4 specifications respectively, whilst category 5 is of a higher specification than that of level 5. These higher grade cables are referred to as **Enhanced Unshielded Twisted Pair (EUTP)** cables providing the improved signal to crosstalk separation required for operation at 16 Mbps and higher.

A.2   Token Ring copper cable connectors

Three types of copper cable connectors are used on Token Ring LANs:

- IEEE 802.5 **hermaphroditic** or media interface connector (MIC)
- 9-way D-type connector for the interface adapter
- 8-way RJ45 connector primarily used on UTP designs.

These are shown in Figure A.2.

D-type connectors (9 and 15 way) are used on several versions of wiring concentrators to provide STP connectivity enabling a greater number of nodes/card to be configured, within the same space, compared with the IEEE 802.5 connectors.

A.2.1   IEEE 802.5 connector

The IEEE 802.5 MIC is available from a wide range of suppliers and is used with Type 1 or Type 6 cable in STP networks. It is designed to enable the cables to be reliably terminated and crimped with the minimum of tools or special skills. A plastic compression nut at the cable entry point holds the cable firmly, once the connector has been fitted, to provide good strain relief. The colour convention of the conductors is based on the IBM colour codes and may not always be valid for cables supplied by other manufacturers.

A.2.2   9-way, D-type connector

The size and mounting arrangements of the IEEE 802.5 MIC make it impractical for connection to adapter cards. The traditional D-type connector is used for this application in STP networks and terminates the adapter cable (Type 6) with a 9-pin, male plug. See Table A.1 for pin connections. The conductors should be crimped, not soldered, and the shield correctly earthed. Plastic and metal versions are available. Whichever type is chosen the cable entry point should be clamped to provide good strain relief.

(a) IEEE 802.5 connector

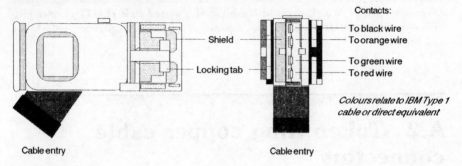

(b) 9-way (9-pin) D-type connector

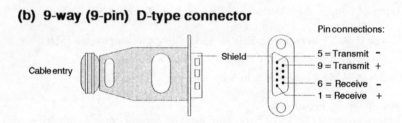

(c) 8-way RJ45 UTP connector

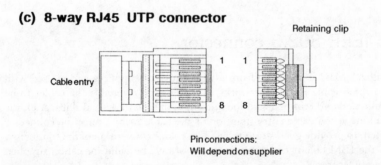

Figure A.2   Copper cable connectors used on Token Ring LANs: (a) IEEE 802.5 connector, (b) 9-pin D-type connector, and (c) 8-way RJ45 UTP connector. The diagrams are not to scale.

Some manufacturers supply adapter cables with premoulded connectors already installed. These ensure good quality terminations and strain relief as the cable sheath is moulded to the plug. However, the plug cannot be removed without cutting the cable, should this be necessary.

Table A.1 Pin connections for Token Ring adapter cable.

9-way, D-type	Signal	Colour (IBM)
1	Receive (+)	Red
6	Receive (–)	Green
9	Transmit (+)	Orange
5	Transmit (–)	Black
2,4,7,8	Signal ground	Not used
3	+5 V	Not used
Shield	Chassis ground	Shield

Colour codes apply to IBM cable. Other manufacturers may use a different colour scheme. The IEEE 802.2 (MIC) hermaphroditic connector uses the above colour codes.

A.2.3   8-way RJ45 connector

The RJ45 connector is the same as that used for telephone applications and, in the same way as the IEEE 802.5 connector on STP systems, is also designed to enable the cables to be reliably terminated and crimped with the minimum of tools or special skills. Cable strain relief is built into the connector, but care should always be taken when handling UTP cabling to ensure that the small and lighter RJ45s are not damaged or pulled free.

Always use high quality RJ45 plugs and sockets. This will ensure that the insertion loss is minimized, the crimp and cable grip are good, and they will last the lifetime of your network.

In UTP network designs the RJ45 connector is used for all terminations except where alternative patching or access points (punch-down blocks) are provided.

RJ14 connectors (4-way) can be used for node connections if only two pairs in the cable are used. *Do not* use RJ14 plugs in RJ45 sockets as this can lead to poor contacts and network errors.

A.3   Fibre optic cables

Fibre optic cables can be used for any and all cable runs in Token Ring networks and can be freely mixed with copper cable segments on the same ring. The properties of fibre, listed below, make it suitable for many applications, in particular for all external cabling where immunity to induced EMF and earth potential differences is essential.

Fibre cables have a number of properties that differ from those of traditional copper cables:

- No electrical signals are passed or induced so they are immune to earth potential differences, lightning strikes and general external (noise) interference (e.g. crosstalk).

- No electrical signals are radiated so fibre complies with security regulations, such as TEMPEST, by default.

- Low loss per unit length. Signals (data) can travel further with less degradation before they need to be reamplified.

- Fibre has a smaller cross-section and is lighter than copper for a given bandwith.

The following application areas are especially suitable for fibre cabling:

- Industrial control.

- Connections between buildings (external).

- General long-distance connections.

- Existing installations with full, or nearly full, ducts. It may be possible to fit fibre into the remaining space but not copper.

- Long, vertical risers. The lighter fibre is easier to install and route than copper.

A.3.1   Types of fibre

Although a number of fibre optic cable designs are in use, the basic construction is one of a central core around which there is a cladding layer and then a protective sheath, as shown in Figure A.3. Most manufacturers classify their fibre cables by specifying

- core/cladding diameters and
- mode of operation.

Core/cladding diameter

The optical signal is carried along the core of the fibre. Around the core is a second layer, the cladding, which is made of similar material to the core but is opaque. The sheath surrounds the first two layers. It is also opaque, and is made of a modern plastic which provides the physical protection. Fibre optic cables with additional protective layers or multiple fibres within a sheath can also be constructed, depending on the application and capacity required.

One of the major parameters affecting signal transmission along the fibre is the core diameter. Commercial fibre cables are available with core diameters in the range 10 to 200 μm (micrometres), with corresponding cladding sizes ranging from 50 to 100 μm wider than the core. The cable size is thus written as 50/125, the first number being the core diameter and the second the cladding diameter, in micrometres.

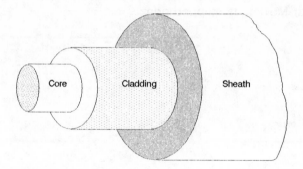

Figure A.3   Typical fibre optic cable construction.

Sheath diameters will vary according to the application and cable type, but will be typically 2 mm or more to provide the necessary protection.

The following cables are the most widely used for local area networks today:

- 50/125 μm, Bell Labs internal standard. This size fibre is also commonly used by the European PTTs.

- 62.5/125 μm, the fibre size adopted for IEEE 802.5 4/16 Mbps and ANSI XT3.9 FDDI 100 Mbps Token Ring networks.

- 100/140 μm, an earlier *de facto* standard not suitable for high speed applications (100 Mbps).

The relatively large core diameters used for local area networks is to enable light emitting diodes (LEDs) to be used for the transmitters as these are less costly than lasers or laser diodes and enable distances up to 3 km between repeaters to be readily achieved. For the longer distance, higher capacity requirements of wide area networks and PTT circuits, lasers are used to drive smaller aperture, very low loss fibre. In this case the core diameter is of the order of 8 μm and inter-repeater distances of 30 km or more are possible.

Operating mode

This describes the way light is propagated along the fibre core. With an LED source the light is non-collimated (the light rays are not parallel to each other) and enters the fibre at a variety of angles, as shown in Figure A.4. When light rays enter the core at a high angle to the axis, on hitting the core/cladding boundary they leave the core and are absorbed by the surrounding material. This is known as **absorption** loss.

Most rays enter the core at a relatively shallow angle to the axis and when they hit the core/cladding boundary are reflected back and along the fibre.

Light travelling at or near the axis will arrive at the distant receiver before light that has been reflected several times from the core/cladding boundary. This intermodal distortion of the signal, as it is known, is one of the factors that limit the maximum distance between repeaters for this type of cable.

(a) Multimode, stepped index

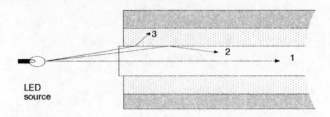

(b) Multimode, graded index

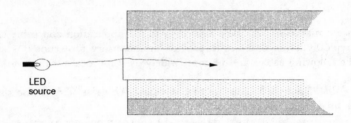

(c) Single mode

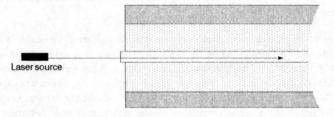

Figure A.4   Modal characteristics of fibre optic cable.

(a) Multimode stepped index fibre:

1. Light beams travelling parallel to the axis pass directly down the core.
2. Light beams hitting the sides at small angles are reflected back into the core.
3. Light beams hitting the sides at larger angles are absorbed by the sheath.

Light beams travelling directly down the fibre have a shorter path than reflected beams, resulting in intermodal distortion.

(b) Multimode graded index fibre:

Light beams are forced into curves by the varying refractive index of the core. This virtually eliminates intermodal distortion.

(c) Single mode fibre:

The very small core diameter only permits parallel mode beams to pass along the fibre core. A laser light source is normally used, to achieve greater distances.

When using a laser source, the light is parallel and of a single frequency. These factors minimize the intermodal and absorption losses and, by using narrow fibres to further minimize the losses, greater inter-repeater distances can be achieved.

The three operating modes for fibre are shown in Figure A.4. They depend on the fibre construction which, in turn, will affect the cost of the fibre cable. In ascending order of costs we have multimode, stepped-index fibre; multimode, graded-index fibre; and single mode fibre:

(a)   Multimode, stepped-index fibre. In this type of fibre the core material has a uniform refractive index, whilst the cladding has a different, uniform, refractive index. Light travels through the core as shown in Figure A.4. Light travelling down the centre of the core (i) has a shorter journey than light that is continually reflected from the cladding (ii). The intermodal distortion thus created for pulsed signals effectively limits the upper frequency (**bandwidth**) of the cable because one must ensure that the time interval between successive pulses is greater than the time delays betweem the extremes of travel modes. Some light will be absorbed (iii).

(b)   Multimode, graded-index fibre. The core material of this fibre has a refractive index that gradually varies from the central axis to the outside edge of the core. The variation is chosen so that light beams furthest from the axis travel faster than the inner beams. The overall effect is to cause the beams to curve back into the core. The refractive index profile is carefully controlled so that intermodal distortion for a specified frequency range can be almost eliminated. The frequency range will be quoted as part of the manufacturer's specifications for the cable. This is the fibre most commonly used on Token Ring local area networks to give high performance, cost-effective transmission. With this fibre, the main limit to inter-repeater distances will be the attenuation of the light as it passes along the core.

(c)   Single mode fibre. In this type of fibre the core diameter and refractive index are carefully combined so that all reflected and absorbed modes are eliminated. Only light travelling directly down the centre of the fibre is propagated. In general, this is the most efficient type of fibre, but requires thinner cores, ranging from 1 to 10 μm. Single mode fibre also uses semiconductor laser sources, rather than the lower cost (eye safe) LEDs used on most multimode systems.

A.4   Token Ring fibre support

Table A.2 shows the range of fibre types that are most commonly used on Token Ring networks. The IEEE 802.5 specifications call for 62.5/125 μm cable, although other core diameters can be used. Single mode fibre is usually not cost-effective for local rings, but for high speed backbones, such as FDDI, **Metropolitan Area Net-**

Table A.2   Cable budgets of commonly used fibre.

Fibre type	Supported	Typical cable budget
100/140 µm graded multimode	Yes	2.5 km
62.5/125 µm graded multimode†	Yes	3.0 km
50/125 µm graded multimode	Yes	2.0 km
Single mode	Not directly	30.0 km

†Recommended on IEEE 802.5 networks.

works (MANs) and the emerging frame relay and fast packet switching networks, single mode fibre is the preferred long-distance carrier medium.

A.4.1   Token Ring fibre connectors

Whereas a competent person can learn to terminate copper cables in a reasonably short time, fibre termination is a skilled job. It is possible to terminate a fibre cable so that it appears to work yet introduces excessive losses and renders the link unreliable. A 0 dB loss connector is not yet available, although in the past few years, new techniques and tools have been introduced which make termination and splicing fibre cables easier, more reliable and require less skill.

For trouble free installation and long term reliability, fibre cables should be installed and terminated only by suitably qualified and experienced companies and full certification of the fibre plant should be obtained before acceptance.

The connector types used on early MAUs may be SMA 905 screw type with a 9 mm straight shank. Although it is possible to use SMA 906 type connectors with a stepped shank on the fibre cable and fit sleeves, this is not recommended because of the possibility of misalignment. The connector types used on current MAUs and wiring concentrators are the ST bayonet type detailed in the IEEE 802.5 specifications.

Connection to/from different diameter cables or between different connector types can be easily accommodated via the patch panels and patching cables. Care should be taken to ensure that the overall loss, from transmitter to receiver, resulting from patching, attenuation and coupling losses, does not exceed the loss budget for the fibre link.

Note that when terminating fibre cables, any fibre protruding from connector ends will damage the lenses in the transmitter or receiver modules. Manufacturer's warranties do not normally cover any damage coused by improperly terminated or incorrectly installed fibre cabling.

A.4.2   Fibre cable budgets

Many suppliers will state the maximum distances they support between directly connected fibre repeaters at 4 and 16 Mbps. In this case they should also specify the cable type, losses and assumed number of connectors and terminations. Alternatively, the installation company may advise on possible fibre lengths for inter-repeater runs depending on the chosen fibre and site details. Before this stage, however, the system planner will almost certainly want to know what typical lengths of fibre are supported in Token Ring networks.

In order to determine the maximum distance between directly connected fibre repeaters we need to know certain details about the fibre and associated components, including

- transmitter power
- receiver sensitivity
- signal absorption by fibre (attenuation)
- connector losses
- transmitter coupling loss
- patches and splices along the cable length.

The transmitter power for typical fibre repeaters is nominally -17 dBm but can vary from -14 to -19 dBm. This value is a function of the emitter characteristics and can change between devices (within specification) and from different manufacturers.

The receiver sensitivity of typical fibre repeaters is nominally -31 dBm, automatically equalizing across the range -7 to -33 dBm to give a Bit Error Rate (BER) of 1 in 10^9. Some fibre receivers incorporate a signal quality monitor which will perform an automatic loopback if the BER falls below 1 in 10^5, for example.

This gives a loss budget of 14 dB (nominal) before the additional attenuation, connector and patching losses are considered.

The signal absorption or attenuation depends on the quality of the cable used, the bandwidth supported and the core diameter. For example, reasonable quality $50/125\,\mu$m cable operating at a wavelength of 820 nm with a 200 MHz/km bandwidth has a 4 dB/km attenuation, whilst a higher grade duplex, zip-cord glass graded-index VW-1 PVC jacket $62.5/125\,\mu$m cable also operating at a wavelength of 820 nm with a 200 MHz/km bandwidth can have an attenuation figure of 2.5 dB/km or less.

In order to calculate accurately the distance between fibre repeaters, the attenuation must be known and, if not readily published, should be verified by the cable manufacturer, supplier or installation contractor.

Connector losses for the SMA (Amphenol) 905 and ST (AT&T) bayonet type connectors can vary from 0.5–2 dB per connector. This will depend on the quality (supplier) of the connectors and their use or, more importantly, their misuse. If fibre connectors are frequently connected/disconnected or otherwise abused, then it is easy to introduce a significant loss at the connector point. Selection of good connectors and their proper use will ensure correct operation even over long fibre cable runs.

Transmitter coupling losses occur between the emitter and the cable connector. The coupling loss is a function of the size of the transmit LED lens and the core diameter of the fibre. If these are matched then the coupling loss is 0 dB. However, if the transmit LED is designed for termination to a $62.5\,\mu$m core and a $50\,\mu$m core cable is used there will be an additional loss of 5 dB. Coupling losses can be increased by poor connector termination and should always be verified, in writing, by the installation contractor.

Patching and splicing along the cable length will increase the losses and hence reduce the available drive distance between repeaters. To achieve the maximum inter-repeater distance, the number of patch cables should be minimized (i.e. a single patch cable) and there should be no splices (i.e. a continuous fibre). Although several splicing kits are now available for joining fibre cables, this still requires a relatively high degree of skill. A good splice may give less than 0.5 dB additional loss but a poor quality splice can increase the losses by several dB.

Note that once the fibre cable has been installed, the final loss budget for each cable run should be verified in writing by the cabling contractor.

Although it is best to determine the exact cable budget, as discussed above, we can calculate approximate values to determine the feasibility of our designs. Some examples are shown below.

Loss budget calculations

Example 1:   Single cable run, one patch, 50/125 μm fibre.

Loss budget	14 dB
Connector losses	2 dB (4 connectors)
Transmitter coupling loss	5 dB
Cable budget	7 dB

If a cable loss of 3.5 dB/km is specified, the maximum cable distance between repeaters will be 2 km.

Example 2:   Single cable run, one patch, 62.5/125 μm fibre.

Loss budget	14 dB
Connector losses	2 dB (4 connectors)
Transmitter coupling loss	0 dB
Cable budget	12 dB

If a cable loss of 3.5 dB/km is specified, the maximum cable distance between repeaters will be 3.4 km.

Example 3:   Single cable run, no patch, 50/125 μm fibre.

Loss budget	14 dB
Connector losses	1 dB (2 connectors)
Transmitter coupling loss	5 dB
Cable budget	8 dB

If a cable loss of 3.5 dB/km is specified, the maximum cable distance between repeaters will be 2.3 km.

Maximum inter-repeater distances can be achieved by reducing the number of fibre patch panels and selecting low loss fibre cables.

APPENDIX B

Planning rules and formulae

B.1 Deriving the general formula

The formulae used in this book to verify our network designs are derived from a single general formula. In this section we will show you how the general formula is derived.

In order for a Token Ring network to work, a single node anywhere on the ring must be able to send a packet round the ring and back to itself, error free, as shown in Figure B.1. The maximum distance any node (typically the adapter card in the PC) can send a packet around the ring in this way is called the drive distance. This will be a function of the drive capabilities of the interface or adapter card, the characteristics of the cable and the rate at which data is transmitted (the data rate). It may be specified by the card manufacturer for a given cable type and network speed (e.g. 4 or 16 Mbps) but more often it will be stated as conforming to *de facto* standard requirements.

The rules, formulae and recommendations in this book can be used with values specified by the manufacturer or, as we have shown in the examples, typical values, giving rise to network designs which most, if not all, products will be able to support.

At least one MAU (wire centre) is required to realize a (physical) Token Ring, hence, from the above definition, any single node attached to the MAU must be able to to send a packet to the MAU and back to itself, error free. The maximum distance from node to MAU in this configuration is called the maximum cable budget (MCB) and is shown in Figure B.2.

If we ignore the loss introduced by the MAU itself (for the time being) we can see that the MCB is equivalent to the drive distance divided by two.

MCB ÷ Drive distance of card ÷ 2

To allow for tolerance and environmental limits, the MCB used in typical lobe length calculations is normally reduced by 10 to 20% of this absolute maximum.

Let us now consider a 2-node network. We will assume that the MCB is 200 m (at 4 Mbps) and that we are using IBM Type 1 cable or equivalent. If both nodes are active (in-ring and repeating frames) and connected to a single MAU then, provided each node is 200 m (or less) from the MAU, the network will work. Why?

177

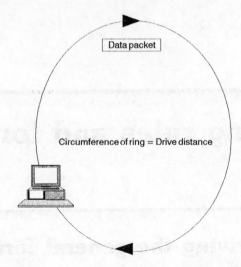

Figure B.1 Example of the drive distance for any node. Any single node (PC) must be able to send a packet round the whole ring and back to itself, without errors.

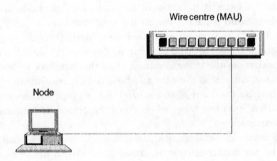

Figure B.2 Defining the maximum cable budget. The most distant node must be able to send a packet to the MAU and back with no errors. The maximum distance from the node to the MAU, ignoring the MAU loss, is the maximum cable budget.

Consider the worst case which is that both nodes are 200 m from the MAU, which is the maximum cable budget, as shown in Figure B.3. When node A sends a packet round the ring it will have to travel a distance of 200 m to the MAU and then a further 200 m to reach node B. Total distance travelled will be 400 m, which is twice the MCB. However, this is the same as the drive distance. Therefore in this worst case example, the data will arive at node B error free because that is how we have defined the capabilities of the nodes.

Now node B will repeat the signal (as do all active nodes) and transmit a new, clean signal back onto the ring. This will be able to travel the drive distance (400 m in this case) to be received at node A error free.

By defining the drive distance and maximum cable budget in this way we ensure that, if all nodes attached to a single wire centre are within the MCB, then

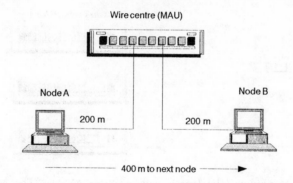

Figure B.3 Nodes at maximum distance from MAU.

any combination of active nodes will always work. These are the basic concepts in Token Ring implementation.

In order to arrive at a general formula that will enable us to verify Token Ring network designs, we need to know what factors affect the maximum distance any node can be from its corresponding wire centre or MAU. This is the maximum lobe length (MLL). These factors consist of the wire centre insertion loss and the cable used to interconnect wire centres, either directly or via wiring closets, as we shall see later.

Wire centre insertion loss

We need to allow for the wire centre loss, that is, the attenuation of the signal as it passes through each wire centre, as each centre added to our network will reduce the MLL by this amount. In the case of a single wire centre the MLL can be expressed as:

$$MLL = MCB - WCloss$$

If we have two wire centres then the MLL might be expressed as:

$$MLL = MCB - 2 * WCloss$$

but this does not take into consideration the cables linking the MAUs together.

We know that a node must be able to drive a signal round the whole ring and back again and when we have more than one wire centre the ring will include the cable between wire centres. Hence the MLL will be reduced by the length(s) of these cables. See Figure B.4. We can therefore allow for the loss associated with each wire centre by expressing the MLL for 'M' wire centres (or MAUs) as:

$$MLL = MCB - K1 * M$$

where K1 is equivalent to the loss of a single wire centre in dBs expressed as an equivalent length of cable, because we want to verify our designs in terms of lobe lengths, plus the length of cable linking two MAUs.

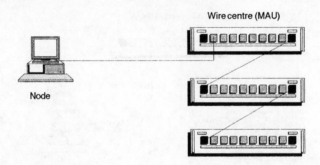

Figure B.4 Maximum lobe length with multiple MAUs. The MLL will be reduced by the MAU loss and the length of cable connecting them.

We include the ring-out to ring-in (patch) cable here so as to simplify the verification process when we have to calculate the MLL for designs incorporating multiple racks and/or multiple wiring closets and because we know there will be one patch cable for every MAU. Note that if a ring is made up of only one MAU – a small network indeed – and the ring-out port is not cabled back to the ring-in port, then the MLL could effectively be increased by the patch cable length. However, as this is only 3 m or less and the values for MCB and the constants in the formula are chosen to give a reasonable degree of tolerance, it is usually ignored.

Whilst some manufacturers express the MLL, drive distances and various network losses in dBs, for the purpose of this book the losses have been translated into equivalent cable lengths. These are then used in the general formula and for the derivations of the formula. We believe this makes it easier to use and understand the concepts and enables you to verify your designs more readily as it calculates the MLL directly in metres.

We can extend the Token Ring by adding more wire centres (MAUs). As long as the wire centres are contained in a single rack, the MLL can be expressed as:

$$MLL = MCB - K1 * M$$

For multiple rack designs and for networks with multiple wiring closets we have to consider the cable linking racks together and linking wiring closets (i.e. the respective wire centres in each rack).

Multiple racks within a single wiring closet

Long patch cables will be used within a wiring closet to link the first and last wire centres in each rack. The interconnection of wire centres in this way forms or makes up the main ring and is called the main ring path. The length of cable used to interconnect the racks of wire centres forming the main ring is called the main ring path length or just the main ring length (MRL). See Figure B.5.

The signal must still be able to go round the whole ring and back to the node, hence the MLL will be reduced by the length of the main ring path leading to:

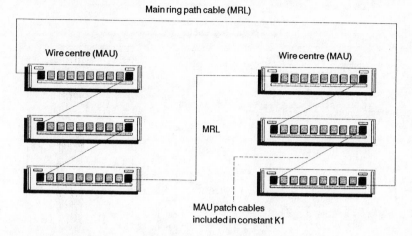

Main ring path cable (MRL)

Wire centre (MAU)

Wire centre (MAU)

MRL

MAU patch cables
included in constant K1

Figure B.5   Maximum ring length for multiple closets.

$$MLL = MCB - K1 * M - MRL$$

for single closet networks with multiple racks.

Wire centres do not have to be mounted in racks. The above formula can be applied to other topologies where wire centres are connected together if the equivalent wire centre loss is known. The MRL then becomes the length of cable directly linking these wire centres.

Multiple wiring closets

In a structured wiring system, communication rooms (wiring closets) are normally interconnected by cables run to/from patch panels mounted in the racks in each closet. The first and last wire centres in each closet will be cabled to the same patch panels and connected to the inter-closet cables (the backbone) by further patch cables. This will introduce additional loss which will be proportional to the number of wiring closets, but need only be considered when *two or more* closets are used.

For designs utilizing two or more wiring closets, the MLL can thus be expressed as:

$$MLL = MCB - K1 * M - K2 * C - MRL$$

where K2 is the loss constant per wiring closet for multiple closet designs and C is the number of wiring closets. See Figure B.6.

The MRL in multiple closet designs will be the sum of the lengths of cable linking wiring closets *plus* all cables linking racks if there are any closets with more than one rack. The patch cables linking individual wire centres are included in constant K1, as discussed earlier.

We have now derived the general formula which can be used for any Token Ring design. As shown in the various examples in the main text, we only need to

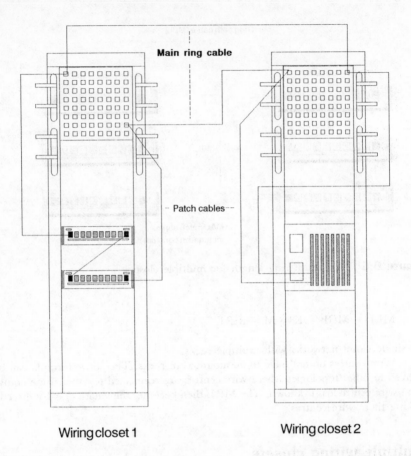

Wiring closet 1

Wiring closet 2

Figure B.6 Main ring (path) length from two (or more) closets. Patch cables connect ring-in/ring-out ports of the MAUs or hubs to the main ring cable via patch panels.

know the values for the different constants (which will depend on the equipment, cable and topology) and we can verify our designs.

The general formula is thus:

$$MLL = MCB - K1 * M - K2 * C - MRL$$

where:

MLL : maximum lobe length
MCB : maximum cable budget
M : number of MAUs (wire centres)
MRL : main ring path length

K1   :   wire centre loss constant

K2   :   inter-closet connector loss constant

C   :   number of wiring closets.

See examples in the main text for using the general formula and its derivatives.

B.2   Summary of planning rules and associated formulae

Now that you have read the book you can use the rules summary below and the specific versions of the general formula to help you verify your network designs. You should be familiar with the accompanying conditions and explanations of earlier chapters in this book. You *should not* use this summary to design networks unless you have read and understood the previous chapters.

B.2.1   Planning rules and formulae for STP networks

Token Ring planning rules for a single ring or ring segment based on shielded twisted pair Type 1 cables

Rule 1   Maximum number of nodes supported per ring is 260.

Rule 2   Maximum number of MAUs per ring is 32.

Rule 3   Maximum number of 8-node MAUs per rack is 12.

Rule 4   Within a rack, connect 8-node MAUs to each other with 3 metres, or shorter, Type 6 patch cables.

Rule 5   Connect MAU lobe ports to the distribution panel within a rack with 3 metres, or shorter, Type 6 patch cables.

Rule 6   Connect MAUs in different racks within the same wiring closet with 10 metres, or shorter, Type 6 patch cables.

Rule 7   Connection from the back of the distribution panel to the wall plate in the work area must be made with Type 1 (or Type 2) cable.

Rule 8   Connections from the wall plate in the work area to the node adapter can use 3 metres, or shorter, Type 6 patch cables.

Rule 9   MAUs installed in a work area should be connected to each other and to wall plates with 3 metres, or shorter, Type 6 patch cables.

Rule 10   All connections between wiring closets and from wiring closets to/from host MAUs in work areas must be made with Type 1 (or Type 2) cable.

Rule 11   All connections between copper repeaters must be made with Type 1 (or Type 2) cable.

Rule 12   All connections between fibre repeaters should use the recommended standard multimode, graded-index fibre of 62.5/125 μm core/cladding diameter.

Rule 13   For networks with copper repeaters, the first repeater pair should be placed at the ends of the longest cable run between wiring closets. The second repeater pair should be placed as far away from the first as possible, at the ends of a cable run between wiring closets, logically opposite the first pair. Networks with more than two repeater pairs should place the repeater pairs at the ends of cable runs between wiring closets such that repeater pairs are equally distant from each other within the practical limitations of the physical network.

Rule 14   Workgroup wire centres mounted in racks in wiring closets must be cabled according to the design rules for host wire centres.

Rule 15   For workgroup wire centres mounted in work areas, the wall plate in the work area must be connected to the ring-out port of the workgroup wire centre using Type 1 (or Type 2) cable for STP network designs.

Rule 16   For nodes connected directly to the workgroup wire centre lobe ports use 3 metres, or shorter, Type 6 patch cables.

Rule 17   Connections from the workgroup wire centre lobe ports to secondary wall plates must use Type 1 (or Type 2) cable.

Rule 18   Connections from secondary wall plates in the work area to the nodes can use 3 metres, or shorter, Type 6 patch cables.

Rule 19   Workgroup wire centres should not be cascaded to form more than two 'levels' of wire centres, including the host wire centre.

Rule 20   The MLL value within a segment bounded by fibre optic repeaters is calculated in the same way as for a segment bounded by copper repeaters and the same rules apply.

B.2.2   Token Ring planning formulae for a single ring or ring segments based on shielded twisted pair Type 1 cables

Single closet networks

Formula A: MLL = MCB – 9 * M – 10 * L

where:

MCB : maximum cable budget

M   : number of wire centres (MAUs)

L   : number of long patch cables.

All distances are in metres.

Multiple closet STP networks without repeaters

Formula B: MLL = MCB – 9 * M – 5 * C – ARL

where:

MCB : maximum cable budget

M   : number of wire centres (MAUs)

C   : number of wiring closets

ARL : adjusted ring length.

All distances are in metres.

  Add 10 to the ARL for every long patch cable in the network including long patch cables between racks in the same closet.

Multiple closet networks with repeaters

Formula C: MLL_n = MCB – 9 * M – 5 * C – Dd_n

where:

MCB : maximum cable budget

M   : number of wire centres (MAUs)

C   : number of wiring closets

Dd   : drive distance for that segment

n : segment number.

All distances are in metres.

  In each segment, add 10 to the drive distance for every long patch cable in that segment, including long patch cables between racks in the same closet.

The segment number will be chosen by the network designer for planning purposes.

Network designs using workgroup wire centres
The maximum lobe length for nodes attached to the workgroup wire centre (MLG) is calculated using Formula D.

Formula D: MLG = MLL – GH – WCloss

where:

MLG	:	maximum lobe length for nodes attached to the workgroup wire centre
MLL	:	maximum lobe length calculated for the network without workgroup wire centres
GH	:	distance from the workgroup wire centre to its connected host wire centre
WCloss	:	workgroup wire centre loss expressed as equivalent length of cable.

All distances are in metres.

For networks without repeaters there will only be one value for the MLL. For networks with repeaters, any segment that includes workgroup wire centres *must* use the value of the MLL calculated for that segment.

B.3   Planning rules and formulae for UTP networks

B.3.1   Token Ring planning rules for a single ring or ring segments based on unshielded twisted pair AWG 24 data grade cables

Rule 1	Recommended maximum number of nodes supported per ring is 100. (Can be increased to 33 MAUs per ring if jitter reduction technology is used.)
Rule 2	Recommended maximum number of MAUs per ring is 12. (See note for Rule 1.)
Rule 3	Maximum number of 8-node MAUs per rack is 12.
Rule 4	Within a rack, connect MAUs to each other with 1 metre, or shorter, UTP data cables.

Rule 5   Connect wire centre lobe ports to the distribution panel within a rack with 3 metres, or shorter, UTP data cables.

Rule 6   Use only one level of patching per lobe cable.

Rule 7   Patch cables/connectors should have a total insertion loss at 16 Mbps of less than 1 dB and a crosstalk better than −35 dB.

Rule 8   Near end crosstalk (NEXT) at the network interface card with UTP cable connected must be better than −35 dB.

Rule 9   Connect MAUs in different racks within the same wiring closet with 10 metres, or shorter, data grade UTP cable.

Rule 10   Connection from the distribution (patch) panel to the wall plate in the work area must use approved data grade UTP cable.

Rule 11   Connections from the wall plate in the work area to the node adapter can use 3 metres, or shorter, UTP data grade cables.

Rule 12   Host MAUs (or hubs) installed in a work area should be connected to each other with 1 metre, or shorter, UTP data grade cables.

Rule 13   All connections between wiring closets and from wiring closets to/from host wire centres in work areas must be made with UTP data grade cable.

Rule 14   Workgroup wire centres must be cabled with the same data grade UTP cable as for host wire centres.

Rule 15   For workgroup wire centres mounted in the same closets as their associated host wire centres, connection from the remote port to the host lobe port must be direct (i.e. not via a patch cable). Connections from the lobe ports of the workgroup wire centre must be cabled the same as the lobe ports of host wire centres.

Rule 16   For workgroup wire centres mounted near their associated nodes, the cable from the host wire centre in a wiring closet to the workgroup remote port will be configured as a normal node cable.

Rule 17   Connections from the workgroup wire centre lobe ports to secondary wall plates must use UTP data grade cable.

Rule 18   Connections from secondary wall plates in the work area to the nodes must use 3 metre, or shorter, UTP data grade cables.

Rule 19   Workgroup wire centres should not be cascaded to form more than two levels of wire centres, including the host wire centre.

Rule 20   The MLL value within a segment bounded by fibre optic repeaters is calculated in the same way as for a segment bounded by copper repeaters and the same rules apply.

B.3.2   Token Ring planning formulae for a single ring or ring segments based on unshielded twisted pair AWG 24 data grade cables

Single closet networks

Formula A: MLL = MCB – 5 * M – 10 * L

where:

MCB   :   maximum cable budget

M   :   number of wire centres (MAUs)

L   :   number of long patch cables.

All distances are in metres.

Multiple closet UTP networks without repeaters

Formula B: MLL = MCB – 5 * M – 5 * C – MRL

where:

MCB   :   maximum cable budget

M   :   number of wire centres

C   :   number of wiring closets

MRL   :   main ring path length.

All distances are in metres.

Add 10 to the MRL for every long patch cable in the network, including long patch cables between racks in the same closet.

Multiple closet networks with fibre repeaters

Formula C: MLL_n = MCB – 5 * M – 5 * C – Dd_n

where:

MCB   :   maximum cable budget

M   :   number of wire centres

C   :   number of wiring closets

Dd   :   drive distance for that segment

n :   segment number.

All distances are in metres.

In each segment, add 10 to the drive distance for every long patch cable in that segment including long patch cables between racks in the same closet.

The segment number will be chosen by the network designer for planning purposes.

Network designs using workgroup wire centres

The maximum lobe length for nodes attached to the workgroup wire centre (MLG) is calculated using Formula D:

Formula D: MLG = MLL – GH – WCloss

where:

MLG : maximum lobe length for nodes attached to the workgroup wire centre

MLL : maximum lobe length calculated for the network without workgroup wire centres

GH : distance from the workgroup wire centre to its connected host wire centre

WCloss : workgroup wire centre loss expressed as equivalent length of cable.

All distances are in metres.

For networks without repeaters there will only be one value for the MLL. For networks with repeaters, any segment that includes workgroup wire centres *must* use the value of the MLL calculated for that segment.

B.4   Token Ring design formulae: table summary

The design formulae are presented for complete at-a-glance reference in Table B.1.

Add 15 m to the relevant value of MCB in Table B.1 for UTP network designs based on level 4 cable or higher (e.g. Systimax from AT&T).

Table B.1 Typical values for STP and UTP formulae.

Data rate (Mbps)	Topology	Shielded twisted pair (1) STP lobe ports	Unshielded twisted pair (2) UTP lobe ports (3)
4	Single closet	MLL < 390 – 9M – 10L	MLL < 200 – 5M – 10L
4	Multiple closet (no repeaters)	MLL < 390 – 9M – 5C – ARL	MLL < 200 – 5M – 5C – MRL
4	Multiple closet (with repeaters)	MLL < 390 – 9M – 5C – Dd	MLL < 200 – 5M – 5C – Dd
16	Single closet	MLL < 180 – 9M – 10L	MLL < 120 – 5M – 10L
16	Multiple closet (no repeaters)	MLL < 180 – 9M – 5C – ARL	Not recommended
16	Multiple closet (with repeaters)	MLL < 180 – 9M – 5C – Dd	MLL < 120 – 5M – 10L (4)

Notes

(1) For IBM Type 1 cable or equivalent
(2) For AWG 24 cable or equivalent
(3) Direct UTP connection to all node ports
(4) Assume repeaters between all closets

General formula for structured cabling designs is

$$MLL < MCB - K1 * M - K2 * C - MRL$$

The values in this table have been selected according to the criteria outlined in this book. Other values of MCB and K1 (wire centre/cable loss constant) can be used, to reflect different topologies, within the limits of the media, data rate and loss levels. All distances are in metres.

Key
L   : number of long cables
M   : number of wire centres (MAUs)
C   : number of wiring closets
ARL : adjusted ring length
Dd   : drive distance (per segment)
MRL : main ring path length
MLL : maximum lobe length

APPENDIX C

Planning forms

Token Ring network design and planning forms are enclosed.
You may copy and use these forms when designing your networks.

Equipment schedule

Designer [ ] Date [ ]

Network no. [ ] Page no. [ ] of [ ]

Item	Part no.	Quantity	Price
PC-bus I/F			
PC/AT-bus I/F			
MCA I/F			
EISA-bus I/F			
Boot ROMs			
Wire centres			
Power supply			
Power supply			
19" racks			
Data cable STP			
Data cable UTP			
Patch cables (3 m)			
Patch cables (10 m)			
Adapter cables			
Fibre optic cable			
Other items 1			
Other items 2			
		Total	

Cable schedule

Designer [   ]   **Date** [   ]

Network no. [   ]   **Page no.** [   ] **of** [   ]

Name	Phone no.	Node address Low 2 bytes	Cable no.	Cable length	From	To

Wiring closet schedule

Designer [   ]   **Date** [   ]

Network no. [   ]   **Page no.** [   ] **of** [   ]

Wiring closet	Location	Qty racks	Interconnection	
			From	To

Rack layouts

Designer [   ] **Date** [   ]

Network no. [   ] **Page no.** [   ] of [   ]

Wiring closet [   ] **Racks** [   ] of [   ]

Rack no. [   ]
MAU1
MAU2
MAU3
MAU4
MAU5
MAU6
MAU7
MAU8
MAU9
MAU10
MAU11
MAU12

Rack no. [   ]
MAU1
MAU2
MAU3
MAU4
MAU5
MAU6
MAU7
MAU8
MAU9
MAU10
MAU11
MAU12

Wire centre sequence chart

Designer [   ] Date [   ]

Network no. [   ] Page no. [   ] of [1]

Wiring closet [   ] Rack no. [   ]

	Ring-in			Ring-out	
From MAU [ ]	Wire centre no. [ ]		[ ] To MAU	
Length [ ]	Longest lobe cable [ ]		Length	
From MAU [ ]	Wire centre no. [ ]		[ ] To MAU	
Length [ ]	Longest lobe cable [ ]		Length	
From MAU [ ]	Wire centre no. [ ]		[ ] To MAU	
Length [ ]	Longest lobe cable [ ]		Length	
From MAU [ ]	Wire centre no. [ ]		[ ] To MAU	
Length [ ]	Longest lobe cable [ ]		Length	
From MAU [ ]	Wire centre no. [ ]		[ ] To MAU	
Length [ ]	Longest lobe cable [ ]		Length	
From MAU [ ]	Wire centre no. [ ]		[ ] To MAU	
Length [ ]	Longest lobe cable [ ]		Length	
From MAU [ ]	Wire centre no. [ ]		[ ] To MAU	
Length [ ]	Longest lobe cable [ ]		Length	
From MAU [ ]	Wire centre no. [ ]		[ ] To MAU	
Length [ ]	Longest lobe cable [ ]		Length	
From MAU [ ]	Wire centre no. [ ]		[ ] To MAU	
Length [ ]	Longest lobe cable [ ]		Length	
From MAU [ ]	Wire centre no. [ ]		[ ] To MAU	
Length [ ]	Longest lobe cable [ ]		Length	
From MAU [ ]	Wire centre no. [ ]		[ ] To MAU	
Length [ ]	Longest lobe cable [ ]		Length	
From MAU [ ]	Wire centre no. [ ]		[ ] To MAU	
Length [ ]	Longest lobe cable [ ]		Length	

Workgroup wire centre sequence chart

Designer [ ]   **Date** [ ]

Network no. [ ]   **Page no.** [ ] of [ ]

Location
  Wiring closet [ ]   **Rack no.** [ ]
or
  Room [ ]   **Position** [ ]

Ring-out

Wire centre no. [ ]	[ ] To MAU
Longest lobe cable [ ]	[ ] Length
Wire centre no. [ ]	[ ] To MAU
Longest lobe cable [ ]	[ ] Length
Wire centre no. [ ]	[ ] To MAU
Longest lobe cable [ ]	[ ] Length
Wire centre no. [ ]	[ ] To MAU
Longest lobe cable [ ]	[ ] Length
Wire centre no. [ ]	[ ] To MAU
Longest lobe cable [ ]	[ ] Length
Wire centre no. [ ]	[ ] To MAU
Longest lobe cable [ ]	[ ] Length
Wire centre no. [ ]	[ ] To MAU
Longest lobe cable [ ]	[ ] Length
Wire centre no. [ ]	[ ] To MAU
Longest lobe cable [ ]	[ ] Length
Wire centre no. [ ]	[ ] To MAU
Longest lobe cable [ ]	[ ] Length
Wire centre no. [ ]	[ ] To MAU
Longest lobe cable [ ]	[ ] Length

Glossary

8218 IBM part number for standalone rack-mounted copper repeater for 4 Mbps only.

8219 IBM part number for standalone rack-mounted fibre optic converter for 4 Mbps only.

8220 IBM part number for standalone rack-mounted fibre optic converter for 4 and 16 Mbps.

8228 IBM part number for standard wire centre or multistation access unit.

8230 IBM part number for intelligent wire centre hub or common access unit (CAU) with in-band management.

Absorption The reduction in the power of a transmitted signal as it travels through the associated medium. Used to describe the attenuation of light as it travels through a fibre optic cable. *See also* Attenuation.

Access control One of the several functional fields within an IEEE 802.5 frame. The access control field of a frame (or token) is the first byte of the physical control field. The access control field contains the priority indicator, token indicator, monitor count and priority reservation fields of the frame or token.

Access priority Prior to transmission onto the ring, frames are queued within the adapter RAM. The access priority of a queued frame is the maximum priority level of the token that the adapter will be able to capture in order to transmit the frame. Queued frames on other adapters on the same ring which have higher access priorities will deny this frame access to the token until no higher access priorities are active on the ring.

Active monitor The active monitor is a special adapter (one per ring on a bridged network) which provides clocking to the ring, as well as other functions such as token error detection and recovery.

Adapter This term is used generally to apply to the Token Ring interface card or network interface card. It can also be used to refer to the Texas Instruments TMS 380 chipset (or equivalent) on the interface card.

Adapter cable Specific network cable which connects the adapter to the lobe cable. This cable has a male DB-9 connector at one end and a standard IEEE 802.5 MIC connector at the other for use on STP networks. This cable has RJ45 connectors on both ends for use on UTP networks.

Address The logical location of a node on the network. Every node on the network must be assigned a unique address in order to communicate correctly across the network. When a node joins an IEEE 802.5 Token Ring, one of the tasks that must be performed successfully is address verification. To assure that duplicate addresses do not occur, a duplicate address test MAC frame is issued by the new node, using its own address as the destination. If any other active node on the ring is using this address, it will accept the MAC frame and the new node will assume that a duplicate address exists. Under these circumstances the new node will not join the ring.

Adjusted ring length (ARL) The ARL is a design term used specifically in multi-closet networks without repeaters. It is the sum of all wiring closet to wiring closet cable lengths less the length of the shortest of these cables.

Allowed access priority (AAP) The AAP is the highest access priority value that a queued frame may use to attempt to capture the token.

ANSI American National Standards Institute. Standards making and approval body.

API Application programming interface, a term describing software interfaces. When developing any application under an operating system, programmers use standard system calls to perform a range of functions (e.g. writing characters to the screen, operating on disk files). PC-DOS has a well documented set of APIs. Novell NetWare offers a range of APIs to facilitate program development and device support. *See* Open Data Link Interface. Alternative APIs for developers of networking software include IEEE 802.2 and NetBIOS (for PC-DOS) plus mail slots and named pipes (for OS/2) and network device interface service (NDIS) for LAN Manager.

Application layer Seventh and final upper layer of the OSI model. If present, the application layer consists of a number of network services such as mail, terminal emulation and remote file transfer.

ATM Asynchronous transfer mode. A technology that supports asynchronous transfer of data at varying transmission rates, using fixed size packets (53 bytes), suitable for carrying digital voice, data and video. For example, an ATM switch with a typical throughput up to 200 Mbps can be used to connect diverse LANs over large areas to realize an ATM wide area network.

Attenuation The difference in magnitude between the transmitted and received signals after passing through a specified network medium.

Attenuation is caused by absorption of the signal within the network medium itself.

AWG   American wire gauge. American standard numbering system for the size of conductors in copper cable. For example, 22 AWG in Type 1 cable is equivalent to $0.324 \, \text{mm}^2$.

Backbone   (1) Core network (usually high speed) to which multiple LANs are connected using routers, bridges or file servers and over which internetwork traffic can pass. (2) On a Token Ring LAN, the trunk cable which connects wire centres (MAUs) and hubs together.

Backplane   Device used to attach and connect interface cards together incorporating multiway slots wired for the transfer of address, data and control information between the connected interfaces.

Bandwidth   The range of frequencies that can pass over a given circuit. The greater the bandwidth of the medium, the more information can be transmitted in a given time period, assuming that the same transmission scheme is used.

Baseband   Transmission of signals without modulation. In a baseband LAN, digital signals are transmitted directly onto the cable (medium) as digital pulses. The entire bandwidth of the LAN is used for one signal. Ethernet, FDDI, IEEE 802.5 and IEEE 802.3 LANs are all examples of baseband transmission schemes.

Baud   A measure of the transmission speed. The reciprocal of the time duration of the shortest signal element in a transmission. *See* bps.

Burned in address (BIA)   The BIA ROM on all Token Ring adapters contains the unique, 48-bit network address expressed as a 12-digit hex number.

bps   Bits per second. Another way (*see* Baud) of measuring data transmission speed. In general, for baseband networks, the data rate measured in bps and bauds will be the same. For networks employing a modulation scheme, the data rate in bps will be a simple multiple of the figure expressed in bauds.

Bridge   LAN interconnection device which operates at the data link layer of the OSI model. In IEEE 802.5 Token Ring networks, source level routing is carried out within the data link layer and allows data to be routed across up to seven bridges. In IEEE 802.3 Ethernet networks, spanning tree bridging is one protocol that enables multiple Ethernets to be connected without having multiple simultaneous links between the same segments.

Bridging router (BRouter)   Device with the functionality of a bridge and router in a single unit.

Broadcast   Delivery of a message to all stations on a given ring or network. The passage of broadcasts across bridges is not normally restricted by the bridge software, although this facility is offered by some vendors.

Routers do not forward local broadcast messages and act as an effective filter to possible 'broadcast storms'.

Broadcast storm A network state of predominantly bridged, CSMA-based networks that occurs when a broadcast packet is repeated a number of times by the active bridges. In extreme cases the resultant broadcast traffic can eventually fill the available capacity of the network.

Bus Backplane of a computer system or electronic subsystem over which address, data and control information is exchanged to enable the attached devices (interfaces) to communicate.

Bus master Interface or device that can take control of a computer bus (usually from the CPU) to transfer data to/from memory.

Common access unit (CAU) – 8230. Intelligent wire centre (hub) from IBM for up to 80 nodes. Network management is provided over the Token Ring LAN (in-band).

Concentrator, wiring (LANs) Multinode wire centre. Term used to describe a wiring unit that supports more than the 8 nodes of the IBM-like MAU, typically on several multinode cards, mounted in a 19 inch chassis complete with power supplies and (some manufacturers) additional management features. *See also* wire centre, hub and MAU.

Communications processor (Token Ring) That part of the adapter circuits responsible for data transfer to/from the host computer and the network.

Contention A dispute between two or more devices for the control of (usually) a communications channel.

Central processing unit (CPU) In any computer system the main controlling processor is called the CPU. Unless it is a multiprocessor architecture, the CPU will also handle arithmetic operations and input/output control.

Cyclic redundancy check (CRC) A characteristic error detection feature of many link level protocols. The integrity of a data field covered by CRC is checked using a polynomial algorithm based on the field content. The result of a CRC is used as a verification parameter between the sender and receiver of the message when directly connected over the same physical circuit. CRCs are not normally propagated through a complex (bridged) network or inter-network, and therefore higher level verification is also performed (at the network and transport levels) to validate the data.

Carrier sense multiple access (CSMA) Contention access method which allows one or more stations to access a single transmission channel. Specific schemes include CSMA/CD (collision detection) which is defined by IEEE 802.3, and CSMA/CA (collision avoidance).

Data link layer The second of the seven layers defined by the OSI model. The data link layer contains the functions for the point-to-point transfer of frames within a single network. Bridges operate from local addresses at the data link layer.

dB (decibel)   Unit of measurement of signal power, named after A.G. Bell. A decibel is one-tenth of a bel. Logarithmic measurement.

Destination   The receiver of a given message or frame. *See also* source.

Diagnostics   Software may also include hardware which is specifically designed to test a piece of equipment. It is often used to assist in the location of faults in the network or in the host interface.

Data-in-wire or dual (pairs)-in-wire (DIW)   Acronym in common use to describe the unshielded twisted pair data grade cable suitable for use on LANs up to 16 Mbps. Typically installed as a 4-pair cable with 24 AWG solid conductors and identified as DIW-4/24.

Direct memory access (DMA)   A method of data transfer between two locations within a computer, normally controlled by the master CPU or a dedicated DMA controller. In the latter case, information is transferred across the host bus with minimum intervention of the master CPU. Bus master devices often use DMA to transfer data.

DOS   Disk operating system. Operating system software for IBM PC and compatible computers.

Drive distance   In a multi-closet network with repeaters, the drive distance replaces the adjusted ring length of multi-closet networks without repeaters. It is defined as the sum of all wiring closet to wiring closet cable lengths within a segment.

Driver   The software code that controls a hardware interface by relaying commands and data to/from the host operating system.

Drop cable   *See* Lobe cable.

Earth potential equalization   A method of limiting ground potential differences within a building.

Enhanced unshielded twisted pair cable   Unshielded twisted pair cable with enhanced crosstalk separation and low attenuation characteristics to enable it to be used on LANs at up to 20 Mbps (possibly 100 Mbps).

Ethernet   Example of a CSMA/CD network. Common term for the most popular CSMA LAN available in three versions, Ethernet I, Ethernet II and IEEE 802.3.

Fibre distributed data interface (FDDI)   ANSI standard for LAN communication based on a 100 Mbps fibre (principally) network, using a timed token rotation protocol.

Fibre optic   A transmission technology that uses light as the signalling carrier. Fibre optic cables can be used as a direct replacement for copper cables in most Token Ring networks. The principle characteristics of fibre optic technology (compared to copper) are its immunity to electrical noise, no radiated signals, longer distances between repeaters and smaller size for a given bandwidth.

File server   Special host on the network which provides virtual disk storage, shared printer services and communications control for participating nodes on the rest of the network.

Frame   Bit pattern which contains control information and data. For a message to be transmitted across a LAN, it is broken down into packets. Control information is assembled and 'wrapped around' each packet prior to transmission onto the LAN. This protocol protected packet is called a frame.

Frame check sequence (FCS)   The FCS is a 32-bit field (Token Ring) which follows the information field of a frame. The FCS contains the CRC which is used to verify the frame integrity.

Frame control (FC)   In a Token Ring the FC field of a frame or token is the second byte of the physical control field. The FC contains a bit pattern which defines the frame as a MAC or non-MAC frame, and the MAC frame attention code. This field is used by the TMS 380 chip-set for frame processing.

Frame format   The order of the control and data fields within a frame.

Frame overhead   A measure of the ratio of the total frame bits occupied by control information to the number of bits of data. Normally expressed as a percentage.

Frame relay   Switching technique which provides a reliable digital pipe for wide area network data transmission without the overhead of OSI Level 2 end-to-end correction, to give improved throughput at typically 2 Mbps. *See also* WAN, SMDS.

Frame status (FS)   The FS field of a frame is the byte appended after the ending delimiter of a frame which is used to denote whether the destination address was recognized and whether the frame has been copied into the destination node's receive buffer. This field is neither code violated nor CRC protected.

Functional address   A type of group addressing which provides a standard address for specialized network devices such as network monitor, bridges and ring error monitor. Up to 31 unique functional addresses can be recognized by the adapter. *See also* group address, broadcast and multicast.

Gateway   A network interconnection device operating above the network layer (4) of the OSI model. A gateway must be used if protocol conversion is required. *See also* bridge, repeater and router.

Group address   A form of multicast address. For LANs, a group of nodes can be allocated a range of addresses such that they have a common, high order (usually) address (e.g. 4000C9BBXXXX). A message can be sent to all nodes in the group by using the high order address for the group, 4000C9BB in this case. *See also* functional address, multicast and broadcast.

Hermaphroditic connector   Also known as the media interface connector. Special type of connector, defined in the IEEE 802.5 standard. Often termed an '802.5 connector'. These connectors are used in all IEEE 802.5 STP-based networks for all connections except the adapter cable host end. The host connection is a DB-9 connector.

Host   (1) Computer system. In a mixed PC/mini/mainframe environment, the term host normally applies to the larger systems rather than the PCs. In LANs, a host can be any attached node. On its own the term does not imply network connection. (2) Wire centre. In a mixed host/workgroup wire centre network, the host refers to the wire centres with both ring-in and ring-out ports which are interconnected to form the backbone or main ring. Workgroup wire centres have only one extension port (ring-out or remote) and attach to node ports of host wire centres.

Hub (LAN)   Access point for multiple connection of nodes. *See also* wire centre, wiring concentrator.

IBM cabling system, cabling plant   A data communications cabling system defined by IBM in April 1984 to encompass future SNA and SAA connectivity products. Cables are defined by type numbers backed up by rigorous technical specifications (e.g. Type 1, Type 2, Type 6).

IEEE   The Institute of Electrical and Electronic Engineers (USA), a standards making body.

IEEE 802   IEEE working committee responsible for the definition of local area network standards. Subcommittees within IEEE 802 are as follows:

IEEE 802.1   coordination and definition of MAC layer bridges
IEEE 802.2   definition of LLC software
IEEE 802.3   CSMA/CD LAN
IEEE 802.4   token bus LAN
IEEE 802.5   Token Ring LAN
IEEE 802.6   slotted ring LAN
IEEE 802.7   Cambridge ring LAN
IEEE 802.8   FDDI LAN.

Intelligent wire centre/concentrator   Advanced wire centre/concentrator from some manufacturers which, in conjunction with their manager software, can be remotely controlled from a single, central management terminal. *See also* wire centre.

Internetwork   A series of networks, linked by routers and bridging routers, which share the same network layer addressing protocol. It is possible to run multiple protocols over the same internetwork but in order for two hosts to communicate they must be using the same protocols unless there is some sort of gateway available to effect protocol translation.

Internetwork layer   The third of the seven layers defined by the OSI model. The internetwork layer contains the functions that enable data to be transferred between any two points on an internetwork of heterogenous local and wide networks connected via routers, gateways or host computers.

Input/output (I/O)   Transfer of data to/from a computer, subsystem or network.

ISDN   Integrated Services Digital Network: an internationally agreed public network offering switched end-to-end digital services.

ISO   The International Standards Organization (Europe).

kbps   Kilobits per second. The prefix for 'kilo' can be shown as upper case (Kbps) or lower case (kbps) to represent 1000.

Jitter   Phase or frequency change from the desired or fixed transmitted value caused by differences in propagation times (delays) of the various waveforms that make up complex (digital) signals. Jitter, when high enough, can give rise to data errors and hence should be minimized or eliminated altogether, if possible.

LAN Manager   Network operating system developed by Microsoft.

LAN Network Manager   Management software from IBM for networks designed with the 8230 CAU.

LAN Support Program   IBM's DOS-based interface software including the driver for the IBM Token Ring cards and NetBIOS to run PC-LAN network software and various emulation packages.

Lobe   The general description for the connection of the host (lobe) to the wire centre. In most contexts lobe, node and host refer to the same connection.

Lobe cable   The cable connecting the lobe to the wire centre or part of same. *See also* lobe length.

Lobe extender   (1) Device (amplifier or repeater) used to extend the length of cable from the wiring closet to workstation (or other node). See respective manufacturer's details for use of and distances supported by these devices. (2) Device to enable more than one node to be connected to a single lobe cable by providing multiple node ports.

Lobe length   The lobe length is an important parameter in Token Ring network designs. It is usually defined as the distance from the wire centre lobe port to the attached PC or host adapter. The purpose of this book is to determine the maximum lobe length that will enable the network to operate with any combination of active hosts. When the recommended cable types and lengths are used for patch cables and adapter cables, the lobe length is slightly modified viz: The lobe (length) cable (which can be made up of a number of interconnected cables) connects to the end of the adapter cable (usually at a wall plate) and terminates at the patch panel in the wiring closet. Then adapter cables connect the lobe cables to the PC (host) adapters and patch cables are used to connect wire centre lobe ports via the patch panel or connector block.

Local area network (LAN) A high speed (typically) data communications system designed to connect hosts within a local geographical area. *See also* MAN, WAN. Voice and video may also be carried over these networks.

Logical link control (LLC) The data link layer of the OSI model is sub-divided into the two layers: media access control and logical link control. LLC is commonly used to refer to the software interface at Level 2, particularly in respect of the IEEE 802.2 interface specifications. *See also* media access control.

MAC frames A class of network frames that carry out the process of the media access control protocols of the adapters. A MAC frame is designated by bits 0 and 1 of the frame control field being reset. In most cases the host processor will not be notified of the transmission or reception of MAC frames. Token-VIEW Plus provides MAC frame management and control (in-band) in addition to out-band intelligent wire centre control.

Main ring path IEEE 802.5 networks are configured in a physical ring (see main text) of interconnected wire centres. When the ring is complete, data travels in a single direction around the ring using only one pair of the two twisted pairs in the data cable. This is called the main ring path. For STP designs, if the ring-in or ring-out MIC connector on any wire centre is unplugged, the connector and associated sockets short the transmit to receive conductors and the signal is then looped back along the previously unused pair in the data cable – also known as the standby ring path. In UTP designs, signal loopback capability is normally provided by switches in the wire centre or concentrator.

Major vector (MV) The MV is the information field of the MAC frame. It consists of a major vector identity and (optionally) one or more subvectors.

Mbps Megabits per second. The prefix 'mega' represents one million. It *must* be shown as an upper case 'M' since a lower case 'm' is the abbreviation for 'milli' which is one thousandth. Transposing these abbreviations is a common error.

Media access control (MAC) The data link layer of the OSI model is divided into the MAC and LLC sublayers. The MAC sublayer controls the services on the adapter which are responsible for correct operation of the ring, including detection of a recovery from error conditions.

Medium/media The medium supports the propagation of electromagnetic energy. Typical media used for LANs include copper cable, fibre cable and infra-red or microwave radiation.

Metropolitan area network (MAN) A communication system (usually high speed) designed to connect LANs (and possibly other resources) within a geographical area such as a town, city, state or country. The general term for this facility is Switched Multi-Megabit Digital Service (SMDS); various systems are under evaluation worldwide by telecommunications operators and manufacturers.

Media interface connector (MIC)   Standard connector for IEEE 802.5 STP networks. *See also* Hermaphroditic connector.

Maximum lobe length (MLL)   The MLL is the maximum distance any node can be away from a wire centre in a single ring network such that the network will work under any combination of active nodes. The purpose of the book is to enable network planners to determine the MLL and ensure their designs will work correctly.

Modulation   The transfer of information by changing the frequency, phase or amplitude of an otherwise stable signal (carrier).

Multistation access unit (M(S)AU)   The term used by IBM and adopted within the industry to describe the 8-node unit that terminates the lobe cables. *See also* wire centre.

Multicast   A controlled form of broadcast. A message that can be received by more than one node on the LAN by the use of some form of address grouping. *See also* functional address, group address and broadcast.

Network Device Interface Standard (NDIS)   A software interface at the data link layer (level 2) for the Microsoft LAN Manager and compatible operating systems; it provides a standard interface to different vendors' network cards. Driver software conforming to the NDIS standard will run on any NDIS compliant version of LAN Manager to provide data transfer and multi-protocol support.

Near End Crosstalk (NEXT)   When data is transmitted on copper cables for which the transmit and receive pairs are in the same sheath, signals can be induced between pairs. This is known as crosstalk. Near end crosstalk results from signals induced in the receive pairs from the transmit pairs close to the transmitter where the transmit signal is usually strongest and the receive signal weakest (i.e. where the cable connects to the LAN card in use – the near end). Screening between pairs and close coupling (twisting together) within a pair can reduce this unwanted crosstalk which can cause data errors, if excessive.

NetBIOS   Network Basic Input Output System. NetBIOS is an extension to the PC-DOS BIOS providing the API for software developers or network applications. Other network operating systems and networking software offer emulation software which allows applications supporting NetBIOS to run in their own NetBIOS environment.

Net BIOS extended user interface (NET BEUI)   The part of the LAN Support Program containing the IBM NetBIOS interface. The other modules of the LAN Support Program include IBM's adapter driver and interrupt routines.

Network   A group of hosts (nodes) joined together by the network media which share the same data link addressing scheme to form a local network. Local networks or resources linked together, either locally or over MANs and WANs, form an internetwork.

Network layer   Also known as internetwork layer. The third layer of the OSI model. The network layer is responsible for the correct transmission (including routing) of packets across an interconnected group of networks or internetwork.

Node   A LAN-attached device with a unique data link address, which is capable of transmitting and receiving messages across the LAN. IEEE 802.5 networks limit the maximum number of nodes on a single ring to 260.

Node dependent (network)   A network in which the length of the cable over which the signal must travel would reduce the signal strength below the level required for reliable reception and where repeaters are not necessarily used to maintain signal levels. Network operation is maintained by ensuring that certain key nodes are always active on the network and these nodes are relied on to repeat the signal. Node dependent networks are *not* recommended for PC-based systems.

Node independent (network)   A network in which the length of cable along which the signal must pass is not sufficient to reduce the signal strength below the reception threshold, or where repeaters are used to amplify the signal in such a way that the network is independent of node activity. Any single station sited anywhere on a node independent network can send signals reliably around the complete network path. Node independent networks *are* recommended for PC-based systems.

Open Data (Link) Interface (OD(L)I)   A software interface at the data link layer (Level 2) for the Novell NetWare operating system providing a standard interface to different vendors' network cards. Driver software conforming to the ODI standard will run on any ODI supported interface to provide data transfer and multi-protocol support.

Open Systems Interconnection (OSI)   The term used to describe the 7-layer data communications model defined by the International Standards Organization (ISO).

OS/2   Network operating system developed by IBM, similar to LAN Manager, primarily for use on Personal Computer Systems PS/2s.

Patch cable   An IBM Type 6 STP or AWG-24 UTP cable used to 'patch' between any two connectors in a wire centre rack. For the purpose of network design, patch cables can be short or long. Short patch cables are always assumed to be 3 m (10 ft) for STP and 1 m (3 ft) for UTP designs; they are used for patching within a rack. Long cables are always assumed to be 10 m (33 ft) or less and are used for patching between racks in the same wiring closet. The network design formulae in this book assume the above lengths for cable budget calculations.

Patch panel A specially designed mounting frame for interconnecting network cable and attached devices, particularly wire centres. Normally mounted in the top half of a standard 19 inch communications rack, IEEE 802.5 style STP patch panels will have holes for 802.5 connectors to fit directly into the panel. Patch panels for UTP networks can either use RJ45 connectors or proprietary connector strips provided they do not introduce attenuation and crosstalk levels beyond those specified. Patch panels are also available for fibre-to-fibre and fibre-to-copper connections.

Phase jitter In order to decode the bit patterns on a Token Ring, participating interfaces have to be synchronized in some manner. As the signal passes along any section of the medium, phase delays, or jitter, accumulate. The IEEE 802.5 ring has an in-built ability to compensate for phase jitter using shift registers. *See also* Jitter.

Physical Control Field (PCF) The PCF is a field which follows the starting delimiter in a frame. The PCF consists of two 8-bit fields: the access control field and the frame control field.

Physical layer The first layer of the OSI model. Corresponds to the physical transmission medium and protocols.

Premises Distribution System (PDS) Cabling architecture and rules to enable buildings to be wired according to a known and accepted standard. Promoted and endorsed by AT&T, initially for telephone installations, the principles have been adopted for local area networks running over UTP. *See also* Systimax.

Presentation layer The sixth layer of the OSI model. If present, the presentation layer is responsible for formatting messages before passing them down to the lower layers of software as well as for reformatting received messages.

Protocol Formal set of rules governing the transmission of data between communicating systems. Different protocols may operate at each layer of the OSI model.

Protocol family A set of protocols operating over the whole range of the OSI model which combine to allow communication between two systems. To achieve successful high level communication, it is essential that the protocols operating within any layer interface correctly with (at the very least) the layers immediately above and below them. A protocol family describes such a coordinated set of protocols. The common characteristic of most protocol families is that at their high level interface they present an API to the host operating system, while at the lowest layer there exists a well documented interface to which dedicated hardware drivers can be written. Examples of complete protocol families include TCP/IP, DecNET and Netware.

Protocol handler (PH) In a Token Ring that part of the hardware and software on the adapter that performs the necessary conversions of the bit streams to/from the ring and adapter card. It is also responsible for the real-time control of the ring protocols, such as CRC generation, CRC checking and address recognition.

PTT   Post, Telegraph and Telecommunications. A general term for any national organization responsible for regulation and control of electronic communications. Thus British Telecom could be described as 'the British PTT' and Deutsche Bundespost as 'the German PTT'. In the USA the regulatory body is the FCC (Federal Communications Commission).

Repeater   A specialized network component which amplifies the network signal. Repeaters are used to maintain signal amplitude independent of the number of active nodes on a network and hence extends the maximum unrepeatered cable distances. Repeaters operate at the physical layer of the OSI model.

Retry   A network event in which a frame is retransmitted in reponse to an error or timeout. Retries will occur a specified number of times, or until the frame is successfully received.

Ring   A network topology in which the nodes (hosts) are connected from one to the other such that data passes through every active node on the ring before returning to the sending node. Physical access to the ring is provided by a wire centre or hub. Wire centres are connected together via ring-in and ring-out ports to accommodate various numbers of host connections. If the last wire centre is connected back to the first then there is a physical ring and, under normal conditions, data only flows in one direction around the ring using one data pair. If the last wire centre is not connected back to the first wire centre so that data is looped back at each end of the ring, then both data pairs in the cable are used. This gives rise to a logical ring albeit from a physical 'string' of wire centres.

Ring interface (RI)   The digital-to-analogue and analogue-to-digital converter from the adapter to the ring. It is possible to provide both shielded and unshielded twisted pair connectors on the adapter card as part of the ring interface.

Ring parameter server (RPS)   The RPS is a host-based function on an IEEE 802.5 Token Ring, which manages key operating parameters of the ring. These parameters are set and updated via MAC level functions.

Ring status register   A 16-bit register used to report the adapter and ring conditions to the attached host.

Ring-In (RI), Ring-Out (RO)   The ring expansion ports provided on wire centres, concentrators or hubs.

Router   A network interconnection device operating at the network layer of the OSI model. The overall collection of networks which are interconnected by routers is known as an internetwork. *See also* bridges, gateways and repeaters.

Routing   The action or process of selecting a series of connections, across multiple networks, to form a communication path between two host systems.

Routing Information Field (RIF)   The RIF is an (up to) 18 byte field found immediately after the source address field in a frame or packet. It is used to store the information required to route packets across bridges to other networks.

Satellite wire centre   *See* workgroup wire centre.

Segment   Portion of the main ring path contained within a repeater pair.

Session layer   Fifth layer of the OSI model. If present, the session layer contains the functions that initiate the communications event, or session, between two network hosts. Network security features including access verification and log in passwords are usually implemented within this layer.

Source   The originator of a frame, packet or message.

Source routing   The routing technique by which hosts are addressed across multiple IEEE 802.5 rings connected by bridges. Called source routing because the routing of a given frame is specified by the source node, not dynamically determined by the network routers.

Spanning tree bridging (STB)   The protocol and algorithms used by many Ethernet bridges to determine the link connections in an Ethernet bridges network. The protocol enables redundant links to be connected and not used for traffic unless the main link fails.

Standby monitor   Any ring adapter currently attached (active) to the ring which is not the active monitor. Only one active monitor can be present at any one time on an IEEE 802.5 ring. In a bridged network each ring will have its own active monitor.

Standby ring path   *See* main ring path.

Star   A network topology in which a central device is used to interconnect host nodes arranged in a 'star' formation, each node having a single dedicated cable. When the central device (e.g. wire centre) is extended to other wire centres, the familiar 'string-of-stars' topology is formed.

Shielded Twisted Pair (STP) cable   In network use it refers to high grade data cable capable of supporting transmission up to 100 Mbps. IBM Type 1 and 6 are examples of commonly used STP cable.

Subvector   Part of the MAC frame major vector.

System command block (SCB)   The SCB is a six-byte buffer used to hold the command to be executed by the adapter and a 24-bit address pointer to a parameter block for the command.

System interface (SIF)   On Token Ring LAN cards it is that part of the adapter circuits providing the interface to the host computer bus.

System status block (SSB) The SSB is an eight-byte buffer used by the adapter to relay status information to the host. Information can be the notification of completed commands, event flags or error codes.

Systimax Trademark of AT&T's shielded (1261/2261) and unshielded (1061/2061) data grade cable with high NEXT separation (better than 42 dB) suitable for digital transmission at up to 20 Mbps.

Throughput The total amount of useful information processed by a specified network component in a specified period of time.

TMS 380 The Texas Instruments IEEE 802.5 chipset. The 4 Mbps chipset is based around five key circuits, while the 4/16 Mbps chipset is based around two key circuits.

Token A special bit pattern used to control access to the ring (or bus) by any node. On ProNET-4, the token consists of 24 bits comprising a starting delimiter (SDEL), access control (AC) and ending delimiter (EDEL) fields. Within the AC field there is a token indicator bit. If this bit is reset, the current frame is the token.

Token bus Broadband bus based, token passing network specified in IEEE 802.4.

Token Ring Usually assumed to be the baseband ring network specified by IEEE 802.5. More generally it is a combined description of an access method and a network topology which applies to a number of network designs, including ProNET, the Cambridge ring, Apollo Token Ring and FDDI.

TOKREUI Formerly TOKen Ring Extended User Interface. IBM-specific link level network software interface providing a standard interface to higher level software. Similar in concept to ODLI and NDIS software modules.

Transport layer Fourth layer of the OSI model. Protocols at the transport layer operate on messages and are responsible for ensuring error free transmissions between any two hosts on an internetwork.

Token Ring Open Integrated Circuit (TROPIC) The Token Ring chipset available from IBM to enable vendors to make plug-compatible Token Ring interface cards.

Trunk cable The cable used to connect wire centres together between wiring closets. Can be IBM Type 1 or 2 (STP) and AWG-24 or Systimax 1061 (UTP).

Unshielded Twisted Pair (UTP) cable In network use this refers to high grade data cable of supporting transmission at up to 16 Mbps. Systimax 1061 and 2061 are examples of UTP network cable.

Wide Area Network (WAN) Generally a public communications system designed to link MANs and/or LANs within a country or world-wide. The most popular WANs use the internationally defined X.25 packet switching protocols but these are usually modified by the national telecoms administration to suit individual country requirements. Private MANs using either X.25 packet switch circuits or dedicated high speed fibre links are also available. High speed networks using fast packet switching techniques are being developed and deployed as are enhancements to existing services (e.g. enhanced 2 Mbps, known as frame relay). *See also* SMDS.

Wire centre (LAN)   Unit designed to allow nodes to attach to a network by providing access, connection and termination of node cables. Wire centres are available in various sizes (node ports) with typically from four nodes upwards. As well as having various sized single wire centres, multiple wire centres can be connected together, via their ring-in and ring-out ports to support more nodes.

Wiring closet   A room designated for communications equipment including racks, wire centres and patch panels. Wiring closets are supplied with mains power in accordance with IEEE 802.5 specifications. Wire centres located in work areas are treated as if they were in separate wiring closets for planning purposes.

Wiring rack   Standard (19 inch wide mounting) communications rack for patch panels and up to twelve 8-node wire centres.

Workgroup wire centre   Special function wire centre from selected manufacturers. The key feature of the workgroup wire centre is that the wire centre and connecting cable to the host wire centre will not join the main ring until there is at least one active node on the workgroup wire centre. When a node joins the ring on the workgroup wire centre, the join ring signal is extended to the associated host wire centre and the workgroup wire centre then joins the main ring. The workgroup wire centre appears as a node to the host wire centre making it possible to add workgroup wire centres to existing networks without effectively extending the main ring cable length. *See also* Lobe extender.

Bibliography

TMS380 Adapter Chipset – Users Guide Texas Instruments Incorporated

TMS380 Second Generation Token Ring User Guide Texas Instruments
   Incorporated

ProNET-10 Network Configuration Guide Proteon Incorporated

IBM Token Ring Network – Introduction and Planning Guide IBM Inc.

IBM Token Ring Network – Installation Guide IBM Inc.

Commercial Building Telecommunications Wiring Standard ANSI/EIA/TIA–568–
   1992

Index